52 Simple Rules
To Improve
Your Relationship

52 Simple Rules To Improve Your Relationship

Tips, Suggestions & Advice From Couples Who Have

Steve Stewart

companion press

po box 2575, laguna hills, california 92654
http://www.companionpress.com
http://www.ImproveYourRelationship.com

.

COMPANION PRESS
PO Box 2575, Laguna Hills, California 92654

Printed in the United States of America
First Printing 2003

ISBN: 1-889138-30-4

52 Simple Rules To Improve Your Relationship:
Tips, Suggestions & Advice From Couples Who Have

http://www.ImproveYourRelationship.com

WARNING

The advice offered in this book is shared in the spirit of hope, inspiration and entertainment and is not intended to take the place of a therapist, psychologist, psychiatrist, medical doctor, lawyer or other professional trained in these areas.

All of the advice, tips, hints, suggestions, solutions and opinions about sex, love, romance and relationship problems offered in this book is strictly the opinions of the individual contributors.

Contributors' advice is based on personal experience that worked for them but may not work for you. Please return this book for a full refund and/or consult a professional if you find any of the advice to be unhelpful or harmful in any way.

This book is dedicated to
unhappy couples everywhere—
may you read this book and learn
to do what happy couples do.

Contents

SECTION 4: The Communication Challenge 62

SECTION 5: The Teamwork Challenge 101

Acknowledgements

First I'd like to thank the thousands of happy couples who have shared their tips, suggestions and advice with me—and the world—over the years. And a special thanks to the many Internet ListServ owners who have allowed me to ask for advice from their subscribers, especially Jeff Laurie at www.sexnewsdaily.com.

I'm also grateful to my daughter Marcia Sanchez for sharing her thoughts and advice which encouraged me to make the book more practical.

My friends have also been of great help: Vinny Percoco for spreading the word and for always being a real cheerleader; Georgene Rada for reminding me that every yin has a yang; Bette Siegel for teaching me to fight fair when we lived together in what seems to be another lifetime ago; to Lori Johnson for her thoughts one sunny day at the beach; to Pamela Payne for generously sharing her experiences and to all my other friends and family for offering their advice, suggestions and most importantly, their ears.

Finally, I couldn't have written this 17th book, not to mention most of the other 16, without the help, encouragement and support of my partner Jim. Living happily ever after for the past 12 years, I have to give him much of the credit for inspiring this book.

Introduction

BEFORE YOU READ THIS BOOK IT MAY HELP YOU TO KNOW WHY I wrote it, who I wrote it for and the 10 questions I'm asked most often about it.

1. What makes this book different from all the other how-to, self-improvement relationship books on the shelves?

To my knowledge, it's the first book that asks the "real experts"—couples already in happy relationships—for their tips, suggestions and advice.

The Rule Book is also designed to be part of a practical three-step program that walks you through improving your own relationship. This is not a book of theory, psycho-babble or simply a so-called experts opinion or agenda.

Once you've read *52 Simple Rules to Improve Your Relationship*, you and your partner may then want to use the companion *Quiz Book* to find out where you need work. Then you and your partner can use the companion *Workbook* to improve your relationship at your own pace, using guided exercises and proven step-by-step techniques.

2. Why did you write this book?

Have you ever wondered why some couples find it so easy to live "happily ever after" while so many other couples live *un*happily ever after, or end up divorced? Me too. That's why I wrote this book.

I wanted to know what happy couples know that unhappy couples don't seem to know.

I believe that if you want to know the secret of getting a job as a newspaper, radio or TV advice expert, the best way is to ask someone who has one of those jobs. Likewise, if you want to know the secret of having a happy relationship, you ask someone who already has one. That's what I did and the result is this book of tips, suggestions and advice.

3. What *do* happy couples know that unhappy couples don't?

There are 10 things that all happy couples have in common. You can read them in Chapter 1, beginning on page 19.

4. What are your credentials? What makes you qualified to write this book? Don't you need to be a therapist to write a book like this?

I'm not a doctor and I don't claim to offer my own advice in this book. For this book I asked as many of the true experts I could find—couples in happy relationships—to share the "secrets," the "keys" and the "rules" they've discovered to having a happy relationship.

This is a book of advice offered by hundreds of happy couples—not doctors or therapists or media personalities. I believe that therapy can be valuable for many couples and essential for some, but I don't believe that every relationship headache requires a therapist. I don't believe therapy needs to be the first resort. In fact, despite the advice of the famous and infamous relationship gurus, doctors and the hundreds of other self-appointed media "experts," divorce rates remain near their all-time highs.

This seems especially odd when you consider that nearly every newspaper has an advice column and every radio station seems to have an advice expert. Is no one reading or listening or is the advice less than helpful?

As for my credentials, I'm a best-selling author who's been writing about sex, love and relationships for more than 20 years. And for 20 years I've been asking, what do happy couples know that unhappy couples don't?

I'm also in a very happy relationship and have been for more than 12 years. When I began this book, I wanted to know if my partner and I were doing something that other couples weren't. In all of these years we've never had a real fight. Are we just lucky? Or, like other happy couples, are we just doing something different? That's what I set out to discover.

5. Who came up with the rules in the first place?

From Adam and Eve to Tom and Nicole, couples through the ages have figured out what works and what doesn't work (based on human nature, common sense, uncommon sense and trial and error) and have passed this timeless wisdom down from generation to generation. These are fundamental and universal rules.

These rules are also reinforced daily in movies, on TV, in song lyrics, at church, in school, at the office and by government. We're constantly exposed to them, so much so, that it's easy to not even notice them, or to take them for granted.

One of the things I've discovered while doing this book is that happy couples are willing to play by these rules, unhappy couples aren't. After receiving tips, suggestions and advice from thousands of couples, I've taken the best responses, and condensed their wisdom into 52 simple rules that any couple can use to improve their own relationship, almost immediately.

6. Why are there 52 rules and not 10 or 100?

In order to make this a practical book, I've condensed the

wisdom of happy couples into 52 simple rules. Many of them could have been lumped together, but I believe it would have been less helpful to readers. Being specific is one of the keys, when trying to solve a problem. I could also have expanded them to 100 or more, but that would only have complicated things and wouldn't have served a useful purpose. The 52 simple rules cover every problem and situation that can arise in a relationship.

7. If the rules are so simple why are relationships so difficult? And why are there still so many divorces?

The simple answer is human nature, for starters. We all prefer to learn from our own mistakes. We complicate things, we misinterpret, and we're skeptical that it can really be so simple. By nature we don't like to follow rules and we don't like to read instructions. Unhappy couples are those who ignore the rules and try to reinvent the wheel.

8. Do the rules work for everyone? Do they work for couples in other countries? Do they work for gay and lesbian couples? How about couples in abusive and addictive relationships?

Yes and no. As long as both partners want to have a happy relationship, they work for any couple. Whether you're straight, gay or lesbian, the rules are the same. Whether you live in the U.S. or China, the rules are the same.

The rules work best if you both have the desire and willingness to be in a happy relationship, but even if only one of you plays by the rules you can still make improvements.

The advice in this book assumes that you both want to improve your relationship. And unless your relationship is based on abuse, addiction, fear or intimidation, it can almost always be improved. If you're in an abusive or an addictive relationship, you don't really have a relationship; you have a hostage situation.

9. If you're an *un*happy couple and you follow the rules, how long does it take to improve your relationship?

According to happy couples, it can happen instantly. Many of the rules are behaviors you can change, or actions you can take immediately.

This book is designed to be practical, so there's one rule for each week of the year. You can improve your relationship week by week or at your own pace. It all depends on you. If you're an over achiever, it may only take you a day. If you take it slow and steady it could take a year. It's up to you how fast or how slowly you choose to go. But one thing is for sure, if you play by these rules you definitely have a greater chance of being one of the "happy couples" than if you ignore them.

10. Why are there so many rules? Isn't following 52 rules, no matter how simple, a lot of work?

According to happy couples, it's all about the small stuff and there's lots of small stuff. That's why there are 52 rules.

Is it a lot of work to follow them? Well, that depends. If you love your job it never feels like work, it feels like a labor of love, it feels like play. The same thing can be said for a happy relationship, the effort can be fun. And if you think of the rules as a game it can also be fun. You also don't have to follow all 52 rules to have a happy relationship; they just increase your odds.

Now, before you dive into the 52 rules you may want to ask *yourself* a few questions.

Would you like to know the four proven ways to get what you want from your partner and to ensure you never have another argument?

Who would you rather ask for relationship advice, a media celebrity trying to be entertaining to sell ads, a therapist who's out of work if you get better, or a couple in a happy relationship?

Are you getting what you want in a relationship? Is your partner?

Do you play by the relationship rules? Does your partner?

What happens if you break the relationship rules?

How many can you afford to break? Which rule should you never break?

Of the 52 relationship rules, how many have you broken this year?

After reading the rules, I'd love to hear from you.

I'd be grateful to know if the rules in this book have helped you become one of the happy couples. Or, if you were already a happy couple, have the rules made you an even happier couple. If you share your personal experiences with me you may even find your personal advice published in future editions of this book or in other relationship books or articles I may write.

In addition, if you have helpful and *specific* personal relationship tips that have worked for you, and you wouldn't mind sharing them with other couples in my monthly *Relationship Tips* newsletter, I invite you to email me at:

email@ImproveYourRelationship.com.

Here's to *your* happy relationship!

Laguna Hills, California
January 1, 2003

10 Secrets All Happy Couples Know ...

that you should know too!

Have you ever wondered why some couples find it so easy to live "happily ever after" while so many other couples live *un*happily ever after, or end up divorced?

Well, you're about to find out. I asked hundreds of true experts—happy couples—to share the secrets, the keys and the rules they've discovered to having a happy relationship.

Much of what they shared seemed obvious, at first. Much of what they shared, however, turned out to be the opposite of what most of us do in relationships—it's what I call uncommon sense.

After talking to and receiving tips, suggestions and advice from hundreds of these couples, I condensed their wisdom into 52 simple rules that any couple can use to improve their own relationship—almost immediately.

So, what do happy couples know that unhappy couples don't? I've discovered that there are 10 essential "smart things" that all happy couples seem to know, or things they do, to "effortlessly" create blissful relationships that unhappy couples simply attribute to dumb luck.

If you want to create your own relationship "smart luck" you'd be well advised to learn the following:

1. YOU BOTH HAVE TO WANT IT
The first thing happy couples know is that you can't have a

happy relationship unless both of you want it. You both have to desire it and be willing to do what it takes. As a couple, you may not even know there are rules, or you may not be very good at following the rules, but if you have a desire and are willing to do what it takes to have a happy relationship, you can have one. But you both have to want it.

You can't force someone who doesn't want to be in a happy relationship to cooperate. The advice in this book assumes that you both want to improve your relationship. And unless your relationship is based on abuse, addiction, fear or intimidation, it can almost always be improved. If your partner is abusive or addicted to a substance, you don't really have a relationship; you have what happy couples call a hostage situation.

UNHAPPY COUPLES rush into relationships and figure they'll fix any problems that may come up later. They believe that if they wish and hope enough that their abusive or addicted partner will become someone else. They pray that he'll become someone who wants to be in a happy relationship. That's if they've given it any thought at all. They often don't know what they or their partner really wants in a relationship and haven't thought to ask, or are afraid that if they do ask they won't hear what they want to hear.

2. IT'S ABOUT BEHAVIORS, NOT FEELINGS

The second thing happy couples know is that it's all about behaviors, not about feelings or personalities. They know it doesn't matter how you feel, as long as you act with kindness and politeness. Often you have to do the opposite of what you think or feel to have a happy relationship.

Happy couples have feelings and emotions too, they just have better self-control or have learned better self-control techniques. They don't allow their feelings and emotions to sabotage their relationship.

UNHAPPY COUPLES are slaves to their emotions and are willing to sacrifice their relationship in order to express their feeling and emotions. They refuse to behave in ways that improve their relationship if it means they must deny expressing their emotions *when* they feel like it.

3. IT'S ABOUT GIVING, NOT GETTING

The third thing happy couples know is that it's not about getting, it's about giving and acting "AS IF." Happy couples give love, affection and support first—even when they're not getting it—because they know it's almost always returned. They act as if they're getting what they want and before long they are.

If you act as if you're happy, you'll soon become happy. Happy couples know that acting as if is the secret to relationship magic.

UNHAPPY COUPLES want to get love, affection and support *before* they will give it. They want proof that you love them before they return your love. Unhappy couples do what everyone else is doing. They follow what seems to be "common sense." Happy couples do the opposite. Their behaviors are often counter-intuitive and make "uncommon sense." What they do is simple, but radical at the same time.

4. IT'S ABOUT THE SMALL STUFF

The fourth thing happy couples know is that it's not about the big stuff, it's all about THE SMALL STUFF! The simple little things you do every day, every week, every month, every year—starting with affection.

In relationships, you have to take care of the small stuff and if you do, the big things take care of themselves. Not the other way around. That's why there are 52 rules in this book. There's lots of small stuff.

UNHAPPY COUPLES think it's all about the big stuff. They focus their attention on the sex, the passion, the "being in love," not realizing that these things are the result of all the small stuff, not the other way around.

5. IT'S ABOUT KNOWING WHAT YOU WANT

The fifth thing happy couples know is that it's important to know yourself, what you want and what you don't want in a mate and in a relationship. And it's equally important to be committed to your "partner wish-list," no matter how lonely or desperate you might be when Mr. or Ms. Wrong knocks at your door and turns out to be a real knock out.

It's not unusual for these couples to have a checklist of things they want and things they absolutely will not accept in a partner and those things they could live with if they had to. Potential partners are checked against the list.

UNHAPPY COUPLES rarely know themselves, what they want or what they don't want in a mate and in a relationship. If they do have a relationship checklist their loneliness or desperation allows them to throw it out the window when Mr. or Ms. Wrong knocks at their door. They often say to themselves that anyone is better than no one and never realize that while they're preoccupied with no one, Mr. or Ms. Right often passes them by, since they're already involved.

6. IT'S ABOUT KNOWING WHAT YOUR PARTNER WANTS

The sixth thing happy couples know is that it's just as important to know your partner and what your partner wants in a mate and in a relationship.

UNHAPPY COUPLES rarely find out what their partner wants in a mate and in a relationship until it's too late. It never even occurs to them to ask.

7. IT'S ABOUT KNOWING THE RELATIONSHIP RULES

The seventh thing happy couples know is that there are relationship rules. And if they don't know what they are, they're willing to learn them. They also know that the rules are not about helping you win at the relationship game. They know that if you win and your mate loses, you both lose. They know it's all about creating a win/win relationship—to get your partner to give you what you want, while at the same time giving your partner what he or she wants.

Happy couples know that the first thing we all ask in any situation or relationship is "What's in it for me?" But equally important, they know that their partner is asking the same question. In other words, in order to be compatible, they know that each partner must get what he or she wants. The relationship must be a win/win situation.

UNHAPPY COUPLES don't even know there are rules. If they did, they would play to beat their partner and to win. They don't understand the concept of a win/win relationship.

8. IT'S ABOUT AGREEING TO PLAY BY THE RULES

The eighth thing happy couples know is that if you don't play by the relationship rules, neither of you can win. THEY AGREE TO PLAY BY THE RULES. If the rules don't work, then they agree to make up new rules that they both can agree on. They know they can reinvent the rules, if they have to, until they're both happy.

UNHAPPY COUPLES refuse to play by the rules. They may try for a while, but give up or decide it's not worth the effort. They need instant gratification. To be fair, it's only human nature to ignore common sense and most rules and to prefer learning from our own mistakes.

Happy couples, however, are able to overcome human nature and our natural impulses. Unhappy couples are not able to do this. Generation after generation they break the rules and try to reinvent the wheel, not to mention, make divorce lawyers rich.

9. IT'S ABOUT NOT GIVING UP

The ninth thing happy couples know is that persistence is often the key to a successful relationship. They know it's important to believe in your relationship and not to give up. They've done their homework and know their relationship is valuable and worth fighting for. If their relationship isn't working, they get resourceful; they try different ways and different techniques and strategies until it begins to work. They get creative.

UNHAPPY COUPLES are instant-gratification oriented and are quick to give up. They often believe it's hopeless and isn't meant to be if it doesn't improve on its own and right away.

10. IT ALL ADDS UP TO COMPATIBILITY

The tenth thing happy couples know is that it's not about love or sex or passion, it's about compatibility. Almost anyone can have sex. And anyone can fall in love. But not everyone is willing to do what it takes to have true compatibility.

Love and sex and passion are never enough to make a relationship work. Compatibility, however, can help make a bad relationship good, and can make a good relationship great. And the good news is, it's not about chemistry or dumb luck. You have the control and you can create compatibility. They know that you create compatibility by making sure you create a win/win relationship. This may seem obvious, but to unhappy couples it isn't.

UNHAPPY COUPLES think it's all about sex, love and passion. Their emotions, intuition and fears guide them. Unfortunately, they also place their bets on chemistry, fate and luck and more often than not, end up losers.

To sum up, if you want your relationship to be a 10, follow these 10 tips and you'll soon join the elite ranks of the top 10-percent of couples in the world—the happy couples.

The Most Important Rule

Follow this simple rule if you want to receive a
Relationship Fast-Forward

#1: The Compatibility Rule

The key to compatibility is in figuring out how to
get what you want, while giving your partner
what he or she wants at the same time.
There are only four ways to do this on your own.

The number one key to a happy relationship is compatibility. The key to compatibility is in figuring out how to get what you want while giving your partner what he or she wants at the same time. In other words, you need to create a win/win relationship.

To happy couples, this is also known as the "Duhhh! Rule," or the "So-Tell-Me-Something-I-Don't-Already-Know Rule."

To unhappy couples, this rule isn't obvious at all. Which is why I've written this book. Each of the 51 rules that follow are about how to do one thing—be compatible with your mate. See, it really is simple.

Okay, so now you're probably thinking, this sounds great, but how do I get my partner to give me what I want, and how can my partner get me to give him what he wants so we can create a win/win partnership?

According to the advice shared in this book by happy couples from around the world, there are only four ways to get your partner to give you what you want, without seeking outside help, such as therapeutic counseling.

The good news is, they're proven techniques that work every time, for couples who want to be in a happy relationship. And if you both use them, you'll never have another fight. You may still disagree, but now you'll be able to solve your disagreements without fighting or arguing.

Now I bet you're thinking, so how come I haven't heard of these techniques before? Well, you probably have, but perhaps not in this context. Or perhaps you ignored them, or didn't think they would really work, or didn't know how to get started.

My partner and I have used them for 12 years and although we may often disagree, we've never had a real fight or argument. They've worked for all of the other couples in this book, as well. If you use these simple techniques, I guarantee the same results for you.

Win/Win Technique #1: Give what you want to get

The preferred way to get your partner to give you what you want is to give it to your partner first. Give to your partner what you most want to receive. Most partners will want to return the favor or gesture.

The problem is most of us do just the opposite. We wait to see if our partner will give us what we want before we offer to give our partner what he or she wants.

You don't wait for a tree to grow or a flower to bloom before you give it water or fertilizer, so why do you withhold the affection, or appreciation or sex in a relationship until you receive it?

Win/Win Technique #2: Ask for what you want

The next best way is to ask your partner for what you want. The problem is most of us want our partner to figure out what we want on their own, as a way of proving their love for us. Either that or we don't think we'll get it and don't want to be rejected, so we don't even ask. Or we don't think we deserve it, so we don't ask. These are just a few of the many self-defeating reasons we don't ask for what we want.

You don't wait until you're starving to death to eat, so why do you wait to ask for what you want only after it's turned into an argument or fight?

For example, if there's something that you want from your partner, that you aren't getting, simply ask her if she can give it to you. She may not have even known that you wanted it.

If she can't give it to you, ask her why and then ask if she can help you figure out a way to get it. When you ask for someone's help, almost everyone is willing to give it.

On the other hand, if you yell, scream, accuse or threaten, under these circumstances almost no one is willing to give you what you want.

Win/Win Technique #3: Negotiate for what you want

The third way is to negotiate or bargain with your partner for what you want. Find out what your partner wants and offer to give it to her in return for getting what you want. We're each motivated by either pain or pleasure, reward or punishment. Once you and your partner know what motivates you, it will make it easier for you to barter.

This technique almost always works.

Win/Win Technique #4: Change what you want

Finally, the easiest way to get what you want is to give up wanting it or change what you want. It's always easier to change yourself than to change your partner. And quite often once you've given up wanting something you realize it wasn't that important to begin with.

The reason I can guarantee that one of these four techniques will work is because you have total control over this one.

If at first you don't succeed, as they say, keep trying. Sooner or later you'll need to master these four techniques if you want to be in a happy relationship. And if not with your current partner, then with your next one, or the one after that. Wouldn't it be simpler to make the effort now?

Section 2
The Shared Values Challenge

Follow these six simple rules if you want
to enjoy Relationship Riches

#2: The Cultural Differences Rule

If you're a fish and you marry a bird, you're likely to have a soggy nest. So make sure you have rubber boots and a raincoat.

It's about behavior, not beliefs

I was very much in love with my first boyfriend but he was a complete chauvinist. Raised in Saudi Arabia, he was taught to believe that women were second-class citizens, with no rights—and put on this earth to serve men—especially him.

Respect for women was not a concept he could grasp. Needless to say, he wasn't my boyfriend for long.

As it turns out, the man I eventually married is also from the Middle East and was raised similarly, but once in the U.S. he altered his behavior and expectations accordingly.

We still have challenges, due to our very different backgrounds, but we both believe that it's our actions and our behaviors that matter, not our beliefs. And *we* act accordingly. Because of this we've been able to have a very happy marriage in spite of our ethnic and cultural differences.

Vivica R., Trenton, New Jersey

It's okay to discriminate, when choosing a mate

My husband Tre is African-American. I'm Spanish. When we first met and fell in love, neither of our families approved. My parents refused to even attend the wedding.

We were both raised in the Southwest but you would think

we were raised on different planets. We've both dealt with discrimination; in fact it's one of the few things we have in common, besides our love for each other. Job discrimination, housing discrimination, police discrimination, educational discrimination, the list seems endless.

Sometimes when you feel the whole world is ganging up against you, you pull together to fight back. There's strength in numbers. In an odd way, pulling together to fight the world has left us little time to fight with one another. Instead, we celebrate every victory, and every year we're still together.

Stephanie W., Oklahoma City, Oklahoma

The key is to embrace your differences with the same affection as you embrace your partner

Tarek was born and raised in Egypt. I was born and raised in Houston, Texas. Our cultural backgrounds and religious beliefs and values couldn't be more different.

We met in college here in the U. S., and fell in love. We knew it would be difficult but decided to marry after we graduated. I think we've had to be more flexible than most couples and more willing to be open to different perspectives.

We're both educators now and I think it helps that we both value learning and new experiences. I believe our different ethnic backgrounds have enriched our lives and made them even happier. And even though it's been more difficult than being in a traditional marriage I'd do it all over again.

The key is in finding your partner's differences enriching rather than annoying or foreign.

Tori A., Dallas, Texas

Some relationships need subtitles

Have you ever watched a movie in English, for instance one from Ireland or Scotland or even England and wished it had

3 3

subtitles, even though you speak English and everyone in the movie is speaking English?

Even within the same country, dialects and accents can be so distinctive that you need a translator. If we can't understand each other, when we speak the same language, how can we hope to understand a partner from a different country, with a different language, different customs, different experiences and different reference points?

It's not always easy, but sometimes it's an advantage.

My wife Sandrine is from South Africa and I believe it's because we're from different cultures that our relationship is successful. There's not much we can take for granted in our relationship so we end up translating for each other. It forces us to be more conscious about what we say and do and how we treat each other. It forces us to question our expectations.

It hasn't always been easy but in an unexpected way this has been the very thing that has allowed us to be happy together. The same thing happens when people from foreign countries come here and do better in school and better in business because they don't take things for granted and are forced to try harder and appreciate what they achieve all the more.

After eight years, we couldn't be happier, while many of our friends, the ones who grew up with similar cultures and who theoretically have it much easier, have divorced or resigned themselves to unhappy relationships.

Andrei Y., New Haven, Connecticut

After reading this chapter, test your relationship I.Q. with the **Improve Your Relationship QUIZ BOOK,** *then use the* **Improve Your Relationship WORK BOOK** *to work on the areas of your relationship that need a little help, using the simple action items checklist in the book. Both books are available only by visiting http://www.ImproveYourRelationship.com.*

#3: The Education Rule

If you want your relationship to bloom, don't forget to pull the weeds and water one another or it's likely to wither and die.

Because it's the smart thing to do

My friend Sandy put her husband through law school and then he left her for a cute, young law clerk.

After 20 years of being a housewife, once all of the kids were out of the house, my mother went back to school. She got her degree and soon after left my father for her professor.

These are just two of many examples I could share about the importance of shared educational values in a relationship.

I've learned from personal experience that education can enrich a relationship or it can destroy it. That's why when my husband decided to go back to school for his master's degree in business, a few years ago, I went right with him.

It was financially difficult but important.

I'm a writer and he's in business, but we're both interested in each other's area. Besides our love for each other, we both value continued education and it's been an important bond in our relationship.

Today, we have many opportunities to combine our interests, which strengthens our relationship each year rather than weakening it. In a happy relationship you never stop learning about yourself and your partner. Learning together is just the smart thing to do.

Monica T., Long Island, New York

Would your partner give you a passing grade?

Having the same educational goals and values is very important if you want to have a happy relationship.

Years ago, when I wanted to go back to school to finish my B.A. degree, my husband Paul was against it. He said it was because our finances were tight, but it turned out he was afraid we'd grow in different directions. I hadn't even considered it, but he was right.

We were both in dead end jobs, with bleak prospects for the future, so we decided that instead of me not going back, he would join me. It was tough financially, but with scholarships and part-time work we pulled it off.

I went back first and got my degree, then it was his turn. We agreed to support each other in reaching our shared goals. I received my B.A. and Paul went on to earn his B.S. degree.

I don't think we'll ever stop learning and I know we'll never stop learning about each other. But the most important thing we learned is that the key to a happy relationship is making sure that you don't do anything—intentionally or unintentionally—that will split it up.

Leanne P., Los Angeles, California

Nearly everyone loves to learn, when the subject is love

My husband Stan and I met in high school. We were very much in love, you know, the kind of first love that seems, at the time, strong enough to overcome all obstacles.

Shortly after graduating, we married. I went on to college and he took a job selling cars. Looking back now, I guess it was inevitable that having chosen such different paths we would grow apart.

I became a teacher and enjoyed the stimulation of the academic life. As the years went by we had fewer and fewer things in common. He began to feel more and more insecure and inferior around my colleagues and at school-related events. It was as if we had separate lives.

Eventually Stan and I divorced and I married a fellow teacher. Bob and I have the same interests, share the same frustrations with our profession and we both value education. I know this is a common story. I've witnessed it many times myself among other teachers. I'll always love Stan, but sometimes love just isn't enough. If he had been interested or willing to continue his education, to grow and to challenge himself, I'm sure we'd still be together today.

Like huge differences in income, a huge difference in education can cause big problems.

Ali Y., New York, New York

After reading this chapter, test your relationship I.Q. with the **Improve Your Relationship QUIZ BOOK,** *then use the* **Improve Your Relationship WORK BOOK** *to work on the areas of your relationship that need a little help, using the simple action items checklist in the book. Both books are available only by visiting http://www.ImproveYourRelationship.com.*

#4: The Fun Rule

Make every day a party and invite your partner as the guest of honor. As much as possible, fill each day with laughter, surprises and planned or spontaneous acts of silliness.

This is not your grandmother's relationship

I remember, like it was yesterday, my grandmother saying to me as a child "you don't have to like your job, you just have to do it if you want to get paid." In her day, the same was true of relationships—you didn't have to like or enjoy your partner, you just had to do whatever you had to do to make it last. That was your reward.

Well, the good old days have been replaced with the fun, fast and fulfilling new days. Now that both men and women work and birth control has freed women from the home, fun and other non-essentials have become an important part of the the relationship equation.

If it's not fun and if the gratification isn't instant, many of us, these days, become bored and restless. There are lots of options today that our parents and grandparents didn't have, but there are still lots of things about relationships that aren't fun—paying bills, housekeeping, getting up in the middle of the night to feed a crying baby and in-law obligations, just to name a few.

My husband Brian and I try to make fun an important and essential part of our relationship. To do this, Brian and I try to turn the unpleasant duties, chores and responsibilities into games, and as much as possible we try to do them together as a family.

For instance, Saturday is cleaning day at our house. One thing Brian does is to hide surprises around the house to be discovered as we clean.

When we visit the grandparents, our kids know that whoever acts the best during the day gets to choose the restaurant on the way home.

Through little things like these, Brian has inspired us. Now, nearly everything we do turns into a fun game, a party or a celebration of something. It's not only made the unpleasant things fun, it's brought us all closer together as a family. It's easy, it doesn't have to cost a thing and you can do it any time, starting immediately. This is our secret.

Laura D., Vancouver, B.C., Canada

Never be too busy for fun

Kevin, my partner of five years, and I make sure to have lots of fun together. If one or both of us have been busy, we take some time to just relax and watch a movie, go for a drive, make stupid jokes, or eat dinner together with candles.

I know that time will be more difficult to find when our new baby arrives, but it's going to be okay, because even a few minutes spent laughing together can really be rejuvenating for our relationship.

Rosalie R., Urbana, Illinois

Crack up to avoid a break up

The best part of my relationship with my husband, for me, and most likely the reason I married him, is his great sense of humor and the laughter we share.

You have to be able to laugh together, to make each other laugh and to laugh at life. It would be too long a road to travel together if you couldn't be silly. And, I especially love it when the whole family is just cracking up at something—those are the best times!

Marcia S., Bakersfield, California

It's hard to be mad at someone when you're both laughing

We've been together for 17 years but I still look forward to coming home each day to Lenny.

Lenny has a great sense of humor and can always manage to put a smile on my face, no matter how stressful my day has been. We have silly pet names for each other, we laugh at ourselves, at each other, at our friends and especially at our families. We still act like kids when we're together.

It's difficult to get too upset with someone you call Pumpkin. And it's difficult to stay mad at someone when you're laughing together every day. This has been the key to our happy marriage.

Dawn F., Cincinnati, Ohio

Warm up your relationship with a few ice cubes

The other night my husband came home late from work. It was dark outside and normally I leave the front porch light on and the house is well lit inside, as I'm usually home. But on this night I kept the lights off and didn't turn the porch light on.

When I heard the key turning in the lock, I hid at the bottom of the stairs, waiting for him to come inside. The door creaked open and that's when I got him. I grabbed my squirt gun and began shooting streams of cold water in his face. He shouted and put his hands up to his face. I laughed my head off as the water gushed all over him. He then dropped his briefcase and chased me around the house. When he caught me, he smothered me in passionate kisses. Within moments we were making love.

I believe the key to having a happy relationship is having fun with each other. Life can be difficult for us, but if we take the time to have fun with our spouse, brighten each other's lives for a few moments, things don't seem so bad.

So, lighten up, grab hold of your partner, give him the biggest hug you can and as you're doing so, stick an ice cube down his pants and you may just warm things up. Hee hee.

Margo F., Tucker, Georgia

After reading this chapter, test your relationship I.Q. with the **Improve Your Relationship QUIZ BOOK,** *then use the* **Improve Your Relationship WORK BOOK** *to work on the areas of your relationship that need a little help, using the simple action items checklist in the book. Both books are available only by visiting http://www.ImproveYourRelationship.com.*

#5: The Lifestyle Rule

A romantic walk in the sand at sunset is more comfortable in bare feet than in high heels. So, make sure you're both dressed for the same lifestyle.

If you take a vacation from love, you'll have your work cut out for you when you return

Todd and I are very compatible, except when it comes to vacations. After a stressful year at work I want to sit and relax by a lake or on a beach and do absolutely nothing for two weeks. Todd, on the other hand, loves adventure and exploration and prefers to spend his vacations white water rafting, mountain climbing or engaged in some other extreme activity. I admire him but it's way too much work for me.

We considered separate vacations but didn't want to be apart for two weeks each year. We enjoy each other's company. So we compromised. We now only vacation in places where we can both get what we want. While he's spelunking down a cave, for instance, I can be sitting under a tree by a stream reading a book and unwinding. And we still have plenty of time to be together in the mornings and in the evenings.

This is just one of the ways creative compromise has helped us to be more compatible over the years.

Lizette H., Washington, D.C.

Sweet, but separate, dreams

When I was growing up we lived on a farm and I was

expected to rise every morning before the sun. My internal clock was always off. I'm a night person, not a morning person and I swore when I left home that I would marry a woman who liked to sleep late. Naturally, I fell in love with and married an early-to-bed, early-to-rise woman. To make matters worse, we're both light sleepers.

After years of conflict, because of our conflicting schedules—I like to stay up late and watch TV in bed, she likes to get up early and read the paper in bed—we came up with a workable solution. We moved into separate bedrooms.

Our friends think it's because we're no longer in love, but nothing could be further from the truth. Our separate bedrooms have brought us closer together.

We've been together now for 10 years. I don't think our relationship would have survived another 10 years in the same bed.

Dylan R., Omaha, Nebraska

Not even the closest couples want to be attached at the hip

I love parties, socializing and large family get-togethers. My husband Craig intensely dislikes parties, socializing and especially large get-togethers. In most other ways we're very compatible, but this has always been a thorn in our sides. Our solution, after many arguments and many events, where neither of us got what we wanted, was to stop trying to force the situation.

I still go to parties, but I now go alone or with a friend, unless it's one of those rare occasions when Craig wants to go along. If I throw a party at our home, Craig either goes out or he participates only as much as he feels like participating. If he wants to go upstairs and watch television during our party, it no longer upsets me.

It took me many frustrating years to realize that just because we're a couple it doesn't mean we're attached at the hip.

Our friends and family think our arrangement is strange but we're happy and that's all that matters in the end.

Serena I., Concord, New Hampshire

After reading this chapter, test your relationship I.Q. with the **Improve Your Relationship QUIZ BOOK,** *then use the* **Improve Your Relationship WORK BOOK** *to work on the areas of your relationship that need a little help, using the simple action items checklist in the book. Both books are available only by visiting http://www.ImproveYourRelationship.com.*

#6: The Money Rule

Love is not a lottery game. Your odds of winning are better if you make sure your relationship checkbook is balanced each month. If you deposit more than you withdraw, you'll keep your partner's interest.

Fortune cookie says: Many receive advice, only the wise profit by it

In the movie comedy *Corky Romano*, Corky (Chris Kattan) drives a bright yellow convertible with a bumper sticker advertising "FREE HUGS—One size fits all." The scene is meant to be silly and over-the-top and to get laughs—which it does. But after watching the movie, it was the only scene that stuck with me.

What if we all advertised and gave away free hugs, free kisses and free back and foot rubs? We all seem to be more than willing to give away free advice to our partners but we suddenly becomes stingy when we have to give them something *they* actually want.

Like affection and sex, money is often an "issue" in a marriage, but I don't think it's really about money most of the time. I think it's about not getting what you really want from your mate. I think we buy things to compensate for what we're not getting, like support, affection, romance and time with our partners. Instead of spending time trying to make more money, we should spend more time giving our spouses what they want. It's easier and worth more in the long run.

My husband Juan and I gave up high paying jobs, a mortgage larger than the annual budgets of some small countries and downsized our lives to be able to spend more time together enjoying our lives. In the process we "supersized" our relationship. Being in an unhappy relationship is expensive. Being in a happy relationship is free.

Brenda A., San Juan, Puerto Rico

You can be financially rich, but relationship poor

One of the primary things that makes our relationship work is that we have common educations and backgrounds. My partner has a degree in engineering, I have a B.S. in applied science/drafting.

He grew up very poor; I grew up poor, but not as poor as he did. Neither of us spends money frivolously. His ex-wife, on the other hand, grew up middle-class and had about anything she ever wanted. She was spoiled and spent a lot of money needlessly. That's a problem they had, that we don't.

This is how we deal with the finances: we split the bills and expenses, beyond that we both save for common items like vacations, and I have my money and he has his. I buy my vehicle, he buys his. We have a joint checking account and we have separate accounts. We have joint credit cards and we have separate credit cards.

Another important factor is that we both have comparable incomes. I think many couples have problems when one person makes considerably more money than the other. It's hard dealing with financial issues when that's the case. With the practical things taking care of themselves, we have more time to take care of each other.

Jenna H., Philadelphia, Pennsylvania

It doesn't cost a thing to be generous to your mate

Money is the issue that causes more trouble to relationships than anything other than communication. To have a happy relationship you need to talk honestly about your budget, spending habits, savings and other money issues.

We make sure we don't make any big expenditures without talking it over with each other first. And we try to remember that if we ask each other's opinion, not to be upset if we don't always get agreement.

There's nothing more pleasing than realizing we've made each other happy or that we truly enjoy each other's company. I've learned that's something money can't buy.

Peggy S., Park City, Utah

Sometimes it's not really about money

One of the things that helped me stay in my marriage of 40 years was becoming a "Born-Again Christian."

I always felt a little put-out not having my own money to buy what I wanted, and I swore if I ever "made it," I would run like hell for freedom.

Well, just before I got my real estate license, I began a personal relationship with the Lord. I worked my butt off and the Lord provided me with lots of money, but by that time I realized that my marriage was more important than the money. It may not work for everyone but it worked for me.

Don't get me wrong, I still have my moments. After all, I'm not perfect, just FORGIVEN. If I make a mistake, or if I'm fresh, or mean, I just ask, "please be patient with me, the Lord's not finished with me yet!"

Joanie D., Elmwood Park, New Jersey

After reading this chapter, test your relationship I.Q. with the **Improve Your Relationship QUIZ BOOK**, *then use the* **Improve Your Relationship WORK BOOK** *to work on the areas of your relationship that need a little help, using the simple action items checklist in the book. Both books are available only by visiting http://www.ImproveYourRelationship.com.*

#7: The Religion Rule

If you want to have a heavenly relationship, pray your partner shares your religious beliefs, views and values. Otherwise, wear cool clothing and be prepared to live in relationship hell.

It's the first rule most children learn and the first rule most adults forget

The Golden Rule is: "Do unto others as you would have them do unto you." Treat others as you would like them to treat you. When we live with someone, we tend to relax and take him or her for granted. We don't think that we need to make the effort to be kind. If you follow the Golden Rule, you'll be easier to get along with, which is important if the relationship is to last. I've found this to be true in my relationship.

Peggy S.,Park City, Utah

Start by practicing religious tolerance at home

Sandy was an agnostic when we met in college. I was an atheist, and still am. About four years into our marriage she became a "Born-Again Christian." Like a reformed smoker, she was intent on converting this sinner and it nearly destroyed our relationship. Fortunately our love was strong enough to pull us through. We both had to learn to respect each other's points of view.

When one partner changes directions in the middle of the journey it can be traumatic for both spouses. But at the same time, once you get past the shock and pain, it can even be interesting.

To me, ironically, the key was faith. Not in a higher power but in our love. When faced with ending our relationship or being tolerant of my different beliefs, she chose tolerance. One of the reasons I fell in love with her in the first place was because she was so tolerant. I prayed in my own way that she would come around and she did.

Jamie R., Boston, Massachusets

Are you in a holier-than-thou relationship war?

The Irish Catholics and Protestants, and the Arabs and the Israelis have nothing on a husband and wife of different faiths fighting over which religion their children will be raised in.

Even if you agree ahead of time, just be aware that once the children arrive, parental instincts kick in and very often you want your kids to be raised with the same religion you were raised with, even if you later rejected it.

This happened to me and my husband Ruben. Ruben was a non-practicing Jew when we married. I was a non-practicing Catholic. At the time, neither of us cared for the restrictions, hierarchy, punitive nature and dogma of organized religion. We didn't imagine it would ever be an issue in our marriage. Then our son Jake arrived and everything changed.

After many battles we came to a compromise but not without a lot of soul searching and difficulty. Religion can be the bedrock of a happy relationship if both partners are of the same faith. But it can just as easily tear a marriage apart if they're not. The key is negotiation—and faith.

Sharon B., New Orleans, Louisiana

Are you on the same spiritual path?

We have some core values that haven't changed in 30

years, or if they have changed it's because we've influenced each other and they've changed to the same degree, in the same direction.

Shared values have served as a foundation for our relationship. For example, I couldn't live with a person whose religious views were at great odds to mine. We were lucky in that we both were brought up Catholic, we were both agnostic when we met, and we have both become atheists since. Had only one of us taken a different route, let's say one of us became a devout Catholic and the other an atheist, I don't think the relationship would have survived.

Bill D., Seattle, Washington

After reading this chapter, test your relationship I.Q. with the **Improve Your Relationship QUIZ BOOK,** *then use the* **Improve Your Relationship WORK BOOK** *to work on the areas of your relationship that need a little help, using the simple action items checklist in the book. Both books are available only by visiting http://www.ImproveYourRelationship.com.*

Section 3
The Shared Goals Challenge

Follow these three simple rules if you want to
enjoy a Relationship Advantage

#8: The Commitment Rule

If your relationship isn't working, try a new strategy. Be creative, have patience and don't give up too soon. Before you give up, think how you would feel if you were the drummer who quit the Beatles just months before they became one of the most successful musical groups in history.

Keep your promises—even if there aren't any witnesses

I feel so grateful for having my partner in my life. We're unmarried by conscious choice, for two reasons. First, because we believe that the legal institution of marriage excludes people for reasons of homophobia; and second, because we believe that our promise to one another is unaffected by who witnesses it, who notarizes it, or what state sanctions it. It's ours alone, a promise based on commitment, trust, communication, monogamy, and deep love for one another.

I think sometimes people marry because they think it will make everything permanent. But successful relationships, married or not, depend on making a promise to one another that only the two of you can fulfill.

Rosalie R., Urbana, Illinois

No refunds and no exchanges

I run a successful mail-order business but it wasn't always successful. Whenever I'm asked my secret to success I always say determination, persistence and commitment.

I knew I had a good product from the start, the rest was all about figuring out how to make the business work. I apply the same commitment to my relationship. I have a no refunds /no exchange policy. All sales are final at work and at home.

I believe that's why my wife and I have had a successful marriage for 16 years—we don't allow ourselves any other option.

Jesse P., Dallas, Texas

In a relationship, H-E-L-P is not a four-letter word

I'm proud of our relationship, but I'm not too proud to ask for help, support and advice.

In order to make it through college I received a scholarship and took out a student loan. When I bought my first house my parents helped me with a down payment. When my wife and I had our first child our parents took turns helping out with the baby the first few months.

I'm grateful for all of the help I've received over the years from family, friends and strangers, alike. Whenever my wife and I have a relationship challenge that we don't know how to overcome, we turn to our friends, our families and if necessary to outside help. With so much support available for couples these days there's no excuse to struggle with a bad relationship alone.

I'm committed to doing whatever it takes to make my relationship work, no matter how embarrassing or uncomfortable it might be. I'm willing to give anything a try. Sometimes all you need is a little help from your friends.

Trent P., Charleston, West Virginia

Commit to your relationship one minute at a time

Buying a home is a major, 30-year financial commitment. Having children is at least an 18-year commitment. Getting a Bachelor of Arts in college is a four-year commitment.

We agree to commit to many things in our lives because

doing so allows us to have the things we want—sometimes in the short-run and sometimes in the long-run.

A commitment to your partner is a lifetime commitment, which may seem overwhelming, but if you just commit to making it better every week, every day and every hour, it's simple.

But before you commit, you might want to start with a one-year subscription to a magazine and see how it goes.

Parker K., Pittsburgh, Pennsylvania

When was the last time you readjusted your relationship portfolio?

Even though my wife Geri and I were never legally married, we exchanged vows at a commitment ceremony 10 years ago in front of our family and close friends and have repeated this ceremony, in a scaled-down version, every year since. For us, a commitment is like an investment in the stock market, but a lot more fun. You need to reallocate and readjust your portfolio every year to make sure you're still getting the returns you require and just to make sure you're still balanced.

Things change, situations change, couples change. We use our yearly anniversary not only to celebrate but to take stock and re-evaluate our relationship and our commitment, and to make sure we're still on course.

Keith J., Chicago, Illinois

After reading this chapter, test your relationship I.Q. with the **Improve Your Relationship QUIZ BOOK,** *then use the* **Improve Your Relationship WORK BOOK** *to work on the areas of your relationship that need a little help, using the simple action items checklist in the book. Both books are available only by visiting http://www.ImproveYourRelationship.com.*

#9: The Family Rule

If your idea of family is *Father Knows Best*
and your partner's is *Mommy Dearest*,
you may end up with *The Addams Family*.
It's always best to compare notes—ahead of time.

Sometimes we already have it all and just don't know it

Like the old saying goes, if your partner walks like a duck, quacks like a duck and looks like a duck, you can try all you want but you'll never turn him into a swan. You'll just turn yourself into an angry, bitter and resentful old goose.

I learned this the hard way and it nearly destroyed our marriage. I married Terry because he was kind, gentle, caring and wanted a family. He loves our kids and is always there to help teach them to swim, or to ride a bike or to catch a ball. He has more patience than I'll ever have. I took all of this for granted and resented him for not trying to get ahead in his career. I blamed him for being passed over for every promotion and for our financial troubles. I made myself miserable and I made him miserable.

I also felt that we weren't keeping up with our friends. We couldn't afford the nice vacations our friends took each year. These were just two of the things I nagged him about.

When our close friends, who spent every summer on a tropical island and every winter at their mountain cabin, divorced a couple of years ago, it was a wake-up call for me. I learned later that my friend's husband, a high-powered executive, had spent most of those vacations on his cell phone or on his laptop computer, working. He worked seven days a week, often from sun up until sun down and hardly knew his own children.

I realized then that I already had what I wanted, what I always said I wanted. The irony is that I found out that all this time my friend had envied me.

Marie G., San Bernardino, California

Make setting your priorities a priority

Tim and I have four boys. We were both single children, raised by single parents. From the start, we both wanted a big family and promised to do everything in our power to make sure our children never had to grow up with only one full-time parent.

I'm a stay-at-home mom and we don't always have the money for all of the things we want or feel we need. But whenever we're stressed or upset with one another, all we have to do is look at our boys and we're reminded of what really matters in our relationship—what our priorities are.

That promise we made, to ourselves and to each other, helps us get through the hard times. I guess it's a commitment that's bigger than any of the daily annoyances and irritations that occur in any family.

In a relationship, it helps to focus on something bigger than yourselves.

Ginny S., Detroit, Michigan

Happily married—without children

Some people have awful childhoods but grow up to have wonderful families of their own. They learn what *not* to do from their parents. I had a horrible childhood and knew from an early age that I didn't want to have children. I made sure to choose a man who felt the same way and we've never regretted not having a family.

Because everyone is programmed by society to get married and have children, if you don't follow the accepted path you become something of an outcast in many circles. Most parents want to associate with other parents. They feel validated and have more in common. It's understandable.

Because of our conscious choice not to have kids we've often had to be our own support group.

If we weren't in agreement on this and able to stand up to the, sometimes intense, peer pressure it would have been much more difficult to combat or ignore.

Knowing ourselves and knowing each other has been our key to a successful relationship.

Kathleen H., Concord, New Hampshire

After reading this chapter, test your relationship I.Q. with the **Improve Your Relationship QUIZ BOOK,** *then use the* **Improve Your Relationship WORK BOOK** *to work on the areas of your relationship that need a little help, using the simple action items checklist in the book. Both books are available only by visiting http://www.ImproveYourRelationship.com.*

#10: The Planning Rule

Some people consult fortune cookies and
fortune tellers to discover what their future holds.
Fortunate couples make their own luck by
planning ahead and following their plan.

**If you warm up, practice for, and anticipate the hurdles,
you can be a relationship champion**

Being in a relationship is like running a hurdle race: just
because you've jumped one "hurdle" doesn't mean you don't
have to jump the others.

Early on in our relationship, Steven and I both thought that
once we dealt with an issue between us, it would be the last
time we'd ever have to deal with it.

It took many years, but we finally came to the realization
that the struggles we had two months into our relationship are
still the ones we deal with after 12 years of marriage.

Our secret to a happy relationship is to always be looking
ahead for signs that a "hurdle" is coming and to prepare for
and anticipate it, rather than blindly stumbling over it.

In our marriage, our biggest "hurdle" has been communication. Our styles could not be more different. When there's a
problem, he withdraws and clams up; I babble like a brook. So
today, when an issue arises that requires intense communication as its remedy, we begin "practice talking" way in advance so when we come upon the actual "hurdle," were both
warmed up and ready to "jump."

This technique has turned what used to be arduous mara-
thon talk sessions, that would last many nights, into com-

fortable, productive, evening dialogues that almost always completely resolves the issue before we turn out the lights and say "good night."

Dianne P., Colorado Springs, Colorado

Plan your divorce settlement before you say "I do" and you'll be less likely to say "I quit"

I think it would be a good idea to have starter marriages, like starter homes. The couple would decide beforehand if they were going to have kids. Then they'd decide what would happen if the marriage didn't work. They'd decide how they'd split things up, who'd get the kids, etc. They'd put it all in writing, have separate attorneys review it for fairness, and then pick a time frame to review and update their plan.

For example, after five years some things may change. If one party decides they don't want to be married anymore, they'd follow the plan. If they both still wanted to be married to each other, they'd make any changes that may be necessary.

It's sort of like a divorce settlement before the divorce. I think people would behave in a more reasonable manner if these things were decided upon prior to the problems starting. And it wouldn't take three years to get divorced.

The attorneys wouldn't make as much money though, which is why it probably hasn't happened. Needless to say, planning has been a big key to our relationship success.

Joy B., Kansas City, Missouri

No one plans to divorce — but divorce can happen if you don't have a plan

My parents divorced when I was 11 and I swore that if I ever married and had children I would never divorce and leave them traumatized the way I was.

No one plans to divorce, but it happens every day. Which

is really my point. You have to plan *not* to divorce or it can easily sneak up on you. It's sort of a marriage default.

When I married my husband Max, we started by making a plan. I believe you plan for the future if you're seriously planning to stay together. My parents prided themselves on being spontaneous free spirits and avoided making plans. I may not be as spontaneous but I take a lot of pride in being happily married — something they never were.

Max tends to be more of a free spirit, as well, so we spend a lot of time negotiating. He'll spend time making plans with me if I spent time having fun with him. So I've just made this part of our plan.

We plan our careers, our educations, our financial futures and a hundred other things, so why not plan to follow your plan? I realize I can be a bit obsessive at times, but my husband helps keep me balanced. Marrying an easy-going, fun-loving man was part of my plan. I knew that if I married someone like me it would never work.

For me, a relationship is like a house under construction. If you want to have the house of your dreams, you need to have a great architect and a beautiful and detailed plan to follow, otherwise there's no telling what it might end up looking like.

Claudia J., Tallahassee, Florida

After reading this chapter, test your relationship I.Q. with the **Improve Your Relationship QUIZ BOOK,** *then use the* **Improve Your Relationship WORK BOOK** *to work on the areas of your relationship that need a little help, using the simple action items checklist in the book. Both books are available only by visiting http://www.ImproveYourRelationship.com.*

Section 4

The Communication Challenge

Follow these 11 simple rules if you
want to increase your Relationship Power

#11: The Agreements Rule

A relationship is a contract, a bond and an agreement. Read the fine print before signing on. Whatever you want is okay, so long as you both agree—ahead of time.

Don't forget to renegotiate on the third Mondays of June and December

Some couples have "understood" rules. Those are the rules the women make up but forget to tell their mates, which usually means he can't be caught looking or standing within fifty feet of where another woman may possibly be standing, especially if she's wearing shoes.

Some of the rules are a little more intricate. For example, "I can step out but you can't," or "We can both step out but we have to tell each other," or "We can both step out but it has to be only on every other Thursday, and my sister's off limits!"

I've discovered that whatever *your* rules are, you each have to agree to them beforehand and then stick to them. Being honest creates trust, no matter what the rules are. And if the rules are acceptable to both parties, then there should be no problems that can't be overcome.

And don't forget to renegotiate on the third Mondays of June and December.

Katrina K., Marmet, West Virginia

Happily agreeing to the terms and conditions of love

For me, one of the most difficult things about being in a

relationship has been having to get my wife's "approval" before I do certain things. When I was single I could do whatever I wanted, when I wanted and with whom I wanted. To continue doing this now would be disrespectful, unkind and inconsiderate, which I don't want to be.

So I've had to learn to become a better negotiator. If I want to go out with the guys on a Friday night I just need to be considerate and let her know enough in advance so she can make her own plans. If it's last minute, she usually doesn't mind, as long as I do something she wants to do at a later date. It's all about bargaining and planning.

It's more work than when I was single but I still get to do most everything I want to do; I just need to plan a little bit better. And if that's all I have to do to be in a terrific relationship with the woman I love, I agree to those terms.

Walker W., Scranton, Pennsylvania

Since only one of you is perfect, it's best to agree to disagree

To get along and to be compatible with your mate you don't need to agree on everything. My husband Todd and I have never agreed about money, about food, about social get togethers or half a dozen other things. We just agree to disagree and then to find a solution that works for both of us.

When it comes to money we pay everything equally, the mortgage, utilities, food, etc. But we maintain separate checking and bank accounts. I like to save money, he likes to spend money. But as long as we cover our mutual expenses, that's all that matters. For example, when it comes to food, he buys what he likes to eat and I buy what I like. Sometimes we share, but it's rare.

If we hadn't agreed ahead of time, I'm sure we would spend much of our time fighting. Instead, we spend most of our time enjoying what we do have in common—that's when

we're not laughing about how peculiar the other one is when it comes to money, food, socializing and on and on.
Bart Q., Miami, Florida

After reading this chapter, test your relationship I.Q. with the **Improve Your Relationship QUIZ BOOK,** *then use the* **Improve Your Relationship WORK BOOK** *to work on the areas of your relationship that need a little help, using the simple action items checklist in the book. Both books are available only by visiting http://www.ImproveYourRelationship.com.*

#12: The Apologies Rule

Think of your partner as a customer and remember, the customer is always right. And if you do, you'll have a loving customer for life. Always be the first to apologize, even if you're right. It's better to be happy than right.

New beginnings often make happy endings

It was one of those stupid fights a couple has after five years of mostly blissful marriage. I had just come home from another long day at work. Of course, as we're a modern married couple, my wife had only gotten home a couple of minutes before me, after her long day at work. And she wasn't pleased. She opened her clenched fist to reveal several candy bar wrappers.

The publishing company I work for had recently offered blood tests to all of its employees. When my results came in, my wife and I were both surprised to see my cholesterol levels so high. Since then, she'd been urging me to eat better. Snickers and Baby Ruths were definitely not on her list.

She said "If you don't want to be around to enjoy our twilight years together, then I don't know why you ever married me in the first place." I didn't know what she was so upset about until I learned she'd been switching healthy products for my usual, fattening ones. But when did she find the time? In between our hectic schedules and long workdays, I could only imagine her getting up half an hour early each morning and stealthily replacing my usual chocolate chip cookies with dietetic ones by moonlight.

Later that night I held her face in my hands in a darkened

movie theater and apologized. She smiled warmly until she saw the bag of popcorn resting gently on my handrail.

"Honey," I explained, "I didn't get any butter on it. And look, it says these Twizzlers are 'low fat'." She looked surprised, if not exactly happy. "Well," she grunted, holding my hand as yet another car chase played out across the giant screen in front of us, "that's a start, I guess."

Not really, I mentally corrected her. It was more like a new beginning.

Rusty F., Orlando, Florida

Love means being the first to say you're sorry

I disagree with the saying, "Love means never having to say you're sorry." That's a little like saying that you never need to water your houseplants!

What love really means is putting the welfare of the other person ahead of your own. That doesn't mean that you always have to do what the person you love says to do. It just means you have to care about their feelings as much as you care about your own.

Peggy S., Park City, Utah

When pig-headed partners fly, pig-headed pride doesn't

When I was younger, I was stubborn and would rarely give in or admit when I was wrong. I prided myself on always being able to win a debate. I was an excellent debater and could argue both sides of any argument. It took me many years to notice that the skill I was so proud of was responsible for ruining so many friendships, work and love relationships.

None of us likes to apologize or admit that we're wrong. It's one of the hardest things to do. I guess that's why it's so effective when we do apologize, because our partner also knows how difficult it is. It took me a long time to learn to apologize and to wise up and realize that you can win all the arguments but still lose the one you love.

My wife Lindsay taught me that relationships are not about winning, they're about loving. She also taught me that it's better to win friends than it is to win arguments.

But even more important, she inspires me to do the things that don't require apologies in the first place.

Dean K., Anchorage, Alaska

After reading this chapter, test your relationship I.Q. with the **Improve Your Relationship QUIZ BOOK,** *then use the* **Improve Your Relationship WORK BOOK** *to work on the areas of your relationship that need a little help, using the simple action items checklist in the book. Both books are available only by visiting http://www.ImproveYourRelationship.com.*

#13: The Arguments Rule

Make regular dates to duke it out. But fight fair
and set the ground rules ahead of time
or you'll find your relationship on the ropes.

Have a rock-solid relationship—in geological time

Howard, my husband of 22 years, is a geologist, so I've learned to look at things in geological time. Whenever we have a problem I ask myself, is that really going to matter in my lifetime, compared to geological time? And it usually isn't. This perspective helps me choose my battles wisely and not sweat the small stuff.
Barbara M., Apple Valley, California

Do you see an elephant? Because I see a tiger

My partner Kevin and I have little code words for when more communication is needed. If one or both of us is stressed a fight can start brewing because we haven't understood each others' needs yet.

If we're just not feeling very in touch, one of us will say, "I think we need a relationship check-in," which is our way of saying, "I love you, so let's get back on the same page." Or, if we're really confusing one another with our behavior, we'll ask, "Do you see an elephant? Because I see a tiger." In other words, we may be looking at the same situation, but seeing two completely different things there.

To give an everyday example, take cleaning the house.

While I'm focusing on making two rooms look good for guests, Kevin may be taking papers from another room and piling them up inside the room I want clean, because he's thinking it's time to get organized.

At times like these, we need to take a break, because Kevin is seeing a tiger in what clearly looks like an elephant to me.

Rosalie R., Urbana, Illinois

They may not be your style, but try on your partner's shoes for a whole new perspective

When we have a disagreement, we either agree to disagree or we talk it out until we're both satisfied with the outcome.

Another thing that's helped us is that we were friends and co-workers for a long time before we got together. We knew each other pretty well and worked together, which enabled us to resolve things without emotion before there were emotional issues to deal with.

Finally, when there's a problem, it always helps to put yourself in the other person's shoes and look at it from their perspective.

Joy B., Kansas City, Missouri

Silence can often sound louder than a scream

I'm a 22-year-old girl and have been with my guy for almost two years now. It hasn't been an easy relationship. Both of us have bad tempers and whenever we used to argue both of us refused to budge.

I soon realized that this just made matters worse. Finally, one day I decided that since you can't fight fire with fire, I'd be the water. So, whenever we'd get into an argument, I'd remain calm and eventually, he would too.

This has worked out really well and now we're much calmer when we talk things over. This method has kind of rubbed off on him as well so now, when I'm angry, he's often the one to give in. So if you're forever fighting, all I can say is, one of you has to be the calm one.

Trust me, if your partner really loves you, he or she will finally be able to see that screaming and fighting doesn't solve anything.

Yuhanies A., Singapore, Malaysia

Remember, you want to win the fight, but you don't want your partner to lose

Every close relationship has some conflict. You need to have a way to resolve these conflicts successfully. I've been married to my husband Charlie for over 20 years and we've learned a few things along the way.

A good place to start is by following the rules for "fair fighting." Don't call your partner bad names, use bad language or violence. Don't bring up things that happened in the past. Don't bring up things that have nothing to do with the issue. Don't try to make the other person feel guilty or stupid or wrong. Don't blow up and then storm off before your partner has had a chance to respond. Explain how you feel without attacking the other person. They're simple to remember and they work like magic.

Peggy S., Park City, Utah

Take a time out or you may run out of time

I believe the key to a happy marriage is communication. You must be willing to give advice as well as receive it. Many situations in a marriage take time and effort and a second look. Often you may be faced with a situation or conflict, but are unsure how to handle it. During these times, you both need to step back, take a deep breath (or even take a walk in the yard or around the block) and come back to reassess the situation. You may find that it truly wasn't that difficult at all to solve, but by taking yourselves away from the current problem and coming back with a new outlook you may find the answer before you.

My husband and I married a year after high school and have been married for 18 years. In that time, we've never gone to bed mad. Yes, there have been times that we've talked until the early morning hours. It also helps to remember the love that you felt when you first met.

I'm happy to say that I practice what I preach and as a result I actually love my husband more today than when I first fell in love with him.

Peggy C., the Internet

After reading this chapter, test your relationship I.Q. with the **Improve Your Relationship QUIZ BOOK,** *then use the* **Improve Your Relationship WORK BOOK** *to work on the areas of your relationship that need a little help, using the simple action items checklist in the book. Both books are available only by visiting http://www.ImproveYourRelationship.com.*

#14: The Expectations Rule

It's okay to expect the sun to rise in the morning but if you expect your partner to live up to your expectations then just as sure as the sun will set at the end of the day, you can also expect to be disappointed.

Create your own relationship reality

Some people are superstitious and some people believe in fate. I believe you get what you expect out of life. If you expect to have a good relationship, that's what you'll have. If you expect to have lots of problems or for it to be lots of work then that's what it will be.

I truly believe we create our own realities and it happens in both conscious and subconscious ways. A positive attitude is everything in life and in a relationship. In every bad or sad or tragic situation you can find something positive if you look for it.

Believing this way doesn't mean you don't have to do anything, that everything will magically happen for or to you. It just means that if there are bumps in the relationship road, you expect to get over them successfully, which in turn inspires you to come up with positive solutions to the inevitable problems that arise for any couple.

No matter how bad your relationship is, imagine and truly believe that the next time you have an argument or problem that the outcome will be positive. You'll be surprised what happens. Even if you have no reason to believe—and nothing in the past would give you reason to believe—have faith, change your attitude first and your relationship will follow.

The secret to good relationships is in knowing that you create it and in knowing that sometimes you have to do the opposite of what you believe will work to allow it to work.
George R., Santa Fe, New Mexico

Well, what did you expect?

It's important to be clear, up front, about what you expect from your partner and to find out what he or she expects from you.

What do you expect? Loyalty? Honesty? Doing half the housework? Which "jobs" does he do? Laundry, cooking three days per week, grocery shopping, cleaning?

Do you expect sex two or three times per week or once every six months? Does your partner want to have recreational sex outside the relationship occasionally? These are things you MUST know before you commit, if you want your relationship to last.

My partner's first live-in girlfriend liked recreational sex with others occasionally. He didn't. That's something I could never tolerate, but some people can. I think that's a big reason he didn't marry her. You need to know about their hobbies and how much time they'll be devoting to them. Does your partner have so many outside interests that there's little time for a relationship? Don't be afraid to ask a few questions up-front or you may not like the answers you receive later on.
Joy B., Kansas City, Missouri

A luxury item a relationship can't afford

Like everyone else, I learned how to be in a relationship from my parents. The problem was my parents were completely dysfunctional. It took me two marriages and a lot of personal work to un-learn everything my parents taught me. I always had unreasonable expectations of my first partner and the relationship. I expected my husband Tony to make me happy, to know what I wanted and to solve all of our problems—after all, what was a husband for?

After causing a lot of needless pain, for my husband, myself and our children, I decided there had to be a better way. But I didn't know what direction to take, so I just gave up. I stopped expecting others to do it for a me and I started taking care of myself and my life turned around.

I'm no longer disappointed by my relationship. I've been remarried for four years now and find I'm rarely disappointed. I've learned that disappointment is a luxury item a relationship can't afford.

Erica V., Springfield, Illinois

After reading this chapter, test your relationship I.Q. with the **Improve Your Relationship QUIZ BOOK,** *then use the* **Improve Your Relationship WORK BOOK** *to work on the areas of your relationship that need a little help, using the simple action items checklist in the book. Both books are available only by visiting http://www.ImproveYourRelationship.com.*

#15: The Fairness Rule

It's not fair to change the rules halfway through the game. It makes it impossible for your partner to win. Don't set boobie traps or land mines. Help your partner to win by starting with an equal playing field.

Look out for land mines

After years of therapy, we can now both laugh about it, but when we were first married, my wife Toni used to set land mines around the house for me to step on. In her mind, if I couldn't figure out what she wanted or needed at any given time, I didn't love her.

Toni didn't trust that anyone could love her, so she set up tests for me that were impossible to pass. This, in turn, only proved to her that she was right in the first place. Her booby traps nearly blew our relationship to pieces. Nothing I ever did was right. She made it impossible for me to love her.

Fortunately, she agreed to therapy and we both learned how to communicate fairly. Fair expectations and fair communication has been the key to our lasting relationship. I have to admit it wasn't easy getting here, but it was worth the effort. And now the only explosions are joyful—and in the bedroom, where they belong.

Vincent G., Queens, New York

If you change the rules in the middle of the game, you both lose

When I met my first wife Bonnie she was a career woman.

We both made very good money, had nice homes, loved to travel and were truly living the good life. We also both wanted a family but didn't want to give up our lifestyles.

When we married and decided to start our family, Bonnie agreed she would go back to work after staying at home with the baby for a year. At the end of the year she decided she didn't want to go back to work, ever. I felt taken advantage of and became resentful. I tried everything I could to get her to compromise, but her decision was final.

We had to scale back our lives and for me it was no longer the good life I had signed up for. Our marriage ended a few years later and I'm now remarried. The lesson I learned is that a relationship can't work if only one partner plays by the ground rules you agreed to going into the relationship. Of course the rules can change over time, nothing is written in stone, but both partners have to agree.

Guy R., Madison, Wisconsin

If you give your partner a test, it's not fair to choose a subject your partner knows nothing about

If you're angry with your partner, for whatever reason, and you don't share this information, your partner is at a disadvantage. It's the same as cheating on a test—you have the unfair advantage.

Okay, so maybe your partner should know that you're mad and should know what he or she did to make you mad, but let's face it, we don't always know when we've done something to anger our partner, even and if we should know—and that's an unfair expectation.

If you're angry—and you want your partner to know it—being passive/aggressive and refusing to share your hurt only makes the situation worse. I know, this was my style for years and it nearly ended our relationship. But before it was too late I realized that holding on to my relationship was more important to me than holding on to my anger, so I started sharing my feelings. I took responsibility for speaking up.

Don't cheat yourself out of a happy relationship by cheating your partner out of all the information he or she needs to make you happy.

Lana J., Bennington, Vermont

After reading this chapter, test your relationship I.Q. with the **Improve Your Relationship QUIZ BOOK,** *then use the* **Improve Your Relationship WORK BOOK** *to work on the areas of your relationship that need a little help, using the simple action items checklist in the book. Both books are available only by visiting http://www.ImproveYourRelationship.com.*

#16: The Initiative Rule

Toot your own horn. And don't be discouraged if
you need a megaphone. Don't expect your partner
to notice all of the things you do for him.
Ask your partner what she wants from your
relationship. Then tell your partner what
you want from your relationship.

**If you want to be on the relationship fast-track you have
to get on the train**

I've been in a happy relationship for many years. In fact,
most of my friends are also in happy and long-term relationships. It's really not that difficult if you just do the same thing
that other happy couples are doing.

Years ago, in business, I learned that those who get ahead,
those who become successful, almost always have a mentor
who shows them the ropes, opens doors and puts them on
the fast-track. You can be successful without a mentor but it
usually takes a lot longer. The same principle works in relationships.

One of our friends refuses to believe this, in spite of all the
evidence to the contrary. He refuses to do what all the rest of
us have done successfully. He refuses to take the initiative to
improve his relationship. He would rather spend his time
complaining about his failures. When I offer him suggestions
or advice it falls on deaf ears.

Even though I'm in a happy relationship, my friend has
never asked me for relationship advice. On the other hand,
my friends who are already in good relationships often ask
each other for advice and share their thoughts about what

makes relationships work.

From my experience, a successful relationship mindset, and being willing to take the initiative to improve your situation, is the key to being on the relationship fast-track.

Wang C., Honolulu, Hawaii

How to get ahead in marriage

I'm a career counselor and I'm always amazed at how few people speak up for themselves, take credit for their achievements, or toot their own horns. It's one of the easiest things we can all do to get ahead in our jobs, but most people expect others to notice or to care about their accomplishments and successes. The sad truth is that most of us are focusing on our own lives and don't have much time to notice or care about someone else's—unless you get their attention.

The successful candidates I speak to all seem to get this. The unsuccessful candidates never do.

I decided long ago to apply the same behaviors that work for my career to my marriage. I would love it if my husband Heath noticed and appreciated every kind, thoughtful and considerate thing I did for him. I'd also love it if he suddenly turned into Tom Cruise, but neither of those fantasies is ever going to come true. So I deal with reality and give him a little help in noticing how wonderful I am.

This is one of those rare cases when selfishness can benefit your marriage. By taking the initiative to make sure he appreciates me I make sure not to let resentment creep into our relationship.

Tamara V., Springfield, Illinois

Little hurts turn into big resentments if you don't speak up for yourself

When you hold in your hurts instead of sharing them

with your partner, right when they happen or soon after, they turn into resentment. Resentment then turns into anger and eventually hostility. If you let it go long enough you end up in divorce court asking "what went wrong," "when did things turn bad?"

I know, this is what happened to my first marriage. I was young and didn't have very high self-esteem. My husband was older and very outgoing and opinionated. I was intimidated and didn't speak up when I felt hurt or taken advantage of. The irony is that most men respect you more for speaking up.

Fortunately I learned from my mistakes and was lucky enough to get a second chance. My husband Brendan is very much like my first husband. I guess I like strong, take-charge guys. But the difference now is that I'm a strong, take-charge gal. Or at least I force myself to be. I speak up for myself and no longer let little hurts turn into big resentments. For me this has been the biggest challenge to being in a relationship and the biggest secret to making it happy. Speak now or forever be miserable.

Molly D., Charleston, West Virginia

Before you send that Dear John letter, send your partner a love note

I just ended a 13-year relationship with a woman and learned a few things, if too late. The most important, don't let the sun set on your bed unless you have worked through whatever is bothering you. If this isn't possible, make a date the next day for discussion.

Don't let another sunset follow. The moment something comes up, deal with it, no waiting. Your relationship is the most important thing on the planet. If you can't say it, write it and ask for a reply. Don't just share your feelings and let them fall to the floor. Make it your first priority, and do it coming from love, not anger. There's nothing so bad that it can't be talked through.

Claire L. J., Maui, Hawaii

After reading this chapter, test your relationship I.Q. with the **Improve Your Relationship QUIZ BOOK,** *then use the* **Improve Your Relationship WORK BOOK** *to work on the areas of your relationship that need a little help, using the simple action items checklist in the book. Both books are available only by visiting http://www.ImproveYourRelationship.com.*

#17: The Knowledge Rule

True or false, if you had to take a relationship pop quiz, would you pass? Do your homework and discover what you and your partner both want from your relationship.

Unspoken communication-style differences can say a lot

Aaron and I have been together seven years and the best thing we ever learned was that we communicate differently.

Silence to him means, "I'm not mad at you. I'm just tired and want to watch TV to unwind before we spend time together."

When I'm silent, however, it means just the opposite: "I'm upset with you and you need to come and hold me and ask what's wrong."

When we finally talked about this, we laughed. Now when he's silent after work I give him his space (and time) to unwind and he knows to comfort me when I become silent and withdrawn.

The irony is that it's improved our relationship to such an extent that neither happens very often anymore. We're so eager to come home from work and share our days that we're now cooking dinner together several nights a week.

Wendy B., Colorado Springs, Colorado

Know thyself or you'll be alone and get to spend a lot of time with a stranger

A friend of mine says she wants to marry an intelligent, hard-working, stable family man. She wants someone she can count on to be there when she needs him. She says she wants a homebody, someone to cuddle with on cold rainy nights. The problem is she only seems to ever date men she meets in leather bars or at motorcycle rallies.

Needless to say, my friend is conflicted—and still single. Either she doesn't really want what she says she wants, or she doesn't believe she can have it.

Before I married Ryan, I was also conflicted. I only dated men with money. High rollers who loved to shower me with expensive gifts, luxury vacations and lots of fun perks, but had little left over for love. For a long time I thought this was the type of man I wanted to marry—until I met Ryan. Let's just say Ryan's idea of a luxury vacation is a two week camping trip in the woods, where you stay in an RV instead of a sleeping bag under the stars. His idea of an expensive gift is a refrigerator.

When we met, I couldn't imagine marrying a man with little money and no real desire to make lots of it. But Ryan made me laugh every day and it didn't cost a thing. He had time to spend with me every day where all of the other guys only had money to spend on me.

No one was more surprised than me to discover that he had all the things I *really* wanted in a man. And in the end I chose love over money and I've never regretted it. I didn't really know what I wanted until I met a man who forced me to ask myself the hard questions. If he hadn't come along I might not have gotten to know what I really wanted until after it was too late. It's never too early to ask yourself what you really want from your relationship.

Diane F., Wichita, Kansas

Make a relationship shopping list

They say that if you don't know where you're going you may not recognize it once you've arrived. I discovered this the hard way.

Everyone wants to be happy, to be loved and to be fulfilled in a relationship. The problem is, from my experience, that few of us take the time to ask ourselves what specifically would make us happy in a relationship. For years I was unhappy, felt unloved and didn't feel fulfilled in my relationship.

My husband Ben is a decent man and a good person, but that wasn't enough. Finally, one day I sat down and wrote a shopping list. But instead of groceries, on the list I wrote down what I believed would make me happy in our relationship. I then asked Ben to make a list of what he wanted. When we compared lists we discovered that neither of us was getting what we wanted.

For the past few years, armed with our list, we've been on a relationship shopping spree. Checking off each item as we accomplish them. I'm not sure if we'll ever complete our lists but I look forward to many years of happiness together as we work towards our new goal.

Maria G., Amarillo, Texas

After reading this chapter, test your relationship I.Q. with the **Improve Your Relationship QUIZ BOOK,** *then use the* **Improve Your Relationship WORK BOOK** *to work on the areas of your relationship that need a little help, using the simple action items checklist in the book. Both books are available only by visiting http://www.ImproveYourRelationship.com.*

#18: The Listening Rule

In a relationship, listen with your eyes and your
heart will hear everything it needs to know.
Just make sure to take off the blinders first.
In other words, actions speak louder than words.

Stop complaining and start listening—with your eyes

Women often complain that men just don't communicate,
that we don't like to talk about our feelings, which is often true.
As men, we're taught to solve problems and to take action.
We're also taught that actions speak louder than words. The
problem is, most women are taught to listen with their ears,
not with their eyes.

I've been fortunate, my wife of the past seven years, learned long ago to stop asking me how I felt and to just observe. I
might not always articulate what I'm feeling, but I always
show it. It's not hard to know how we, as men, feel. We show it
every day by what we do.

Over the years my wife and I have come to meet in the
middle. I try to remember to tell her how I'm feeling, especially
if I'm angry or hurt, and she tries to remember to pay attention
and notice what I'm saying, with my actions. This one thing
has made all the difference in our relationship.

Martin L., Sterling Heights, Michigan

Use a megaphone if you have to

We've been lucky. My husband Justin and I have had few
arguments over the years. When we do fight it's usually a

result of having not listened to each other, or having not heard each other.

Justin has always had a bad habit of telling me something important when I'm distracted, in the other room, or as he's on his way out the door. Later on, when I don't remember something he's told me, or perhaps something I never even heard in the first place, he gets angry and says I never listened to him.

We now have an agreement that if either of us has something to say, and truly wants the other person to hear it or remember it, it's the speaker's responsibility to make sure that happens, not the listener's. That means if I have something important to say to Justin I make sure I have his undivided attention. Then I ask him to repeat it to make sure he hears me. And he does the same with me.

Now, when either of us jokes "you'll be tested on this later," we know it's important to the other that we stop what we're doing and listen. It's a simple technique, but it's solved the problem.

Sylvia J., Sacramento, California

Listen to the old adage that states we have one mouth and two ears because God meant for us to listen twice as much as we speak

To have a happy relationship we first have to learn to listen to ourselves. Listening to ourselves and learning to read our own signals is the first step towards listening and appreciating the tacit clues emanating from our spouses about their needs and desires.

Secondly, we have to learn to read between the lines of speech to the meaning within the silences. When our partner is quiet, is it a healthy quiet, one suffused with calm contentment, or is it fraught with tension? Is there nothing to discuss or is denial easier than a frank discussion of the issue at hand? Is our partner telling us only what we want to hear?

Our ancestors, despite the lack of household innovations and technology, had the time to listen to each other. There were no distractions like cable and e-mail. It's much more difficult today, which is perhaps why relationships are more difficult.

To have a happy relationship, it's necessary to make time for quiet contemplation and communion with your spouse. This has been our secret.

It's when we're silent that we say the most about how much we care. Enough said?

Chave K., Brooklyn, New York

Are you just hearing what you want to hear?

I learned years ago that active listening means to listen to what your partner is saying and then restate back to your partner what you think you've just heard. This gives your partner an opportunity to correct your understanding if it's faulty. It's surprising how often we hear what we want, positive or negative, not what is actually said.

Peggy S., Park City, Utah

After reading this chapter, test your relationship I.Q. with the **Improve Your Relationship QUIZ BOOK,** *then use the* **Improve Your Relationship WORK BOOK** *to work on the areas of your relationship that need a little help, using the simple action items checklist in the book. Both books are available only by visiting http://www.ImproveYourRelationship.com.*

#19: The Sharing Rule

If you want someone to read your mind,
consult a psychic—don't expect
your partner to do it.

When you were a child, adults likely taught you it was important to share, but they probably forgot to mention that it's even more important to share, once you're an adult

One key to a long and happy relationship is to share fun activities together. Our grown son lives in a condo with a pool that allows guests. In the summer, my husband Robert and I spend one to two afternoons a week at the pool. We swim, we talk, we relax together. We have a wonderful time. It's also important to not just sit home and watch TV every night. We talk to each other. We share what we did during the day, our concerns, our joys. It's a joy to be with someone who shares.
Bea S., Manchester, Connecticut

Are you asking the right questions?

The biggest complaint most women have is that men don't share their feelings. I know, I was one of those women.

"Feelings" is a very big topic and most men just don't know where to start. Sometimes they need a little coaching. I think sometimes we forget that they're not women. We can talk about every aspect of feelings, from every possible angle and perspective and never run out of things to say.

With my husband, Lance, I've discovered that if I ask a

very specific question, rather than general questions, I can usually get him to open up about his feelings.

For instance, if he comes home from work angry or frustrated or withdrawn, if I ask "What's wrong?" he'll usually just say "Nothing" or "I just had a rotten day" and leave it at that. Instead, if I ask "Did someone at work piss you off today," he'll either say "Yes" and then begin explaining and sharing what happened, or he'll say "no." If he says "no" I just keep probing. I say "Oh, did you get saddled with another rush project?" Or "Did so and so take all the credit for your work again?"

After the second or third question, he knows I'm interested in knowing the specific details of what caused him to be in the mood he's in. Once he begins talking, he usually opens up about other things. He asks about my day and we end up having a meaningful discussion.

Most men are willing to share their feelings. You just need to ask the right questions in the right way and get the ball rolling.

Mia J., Albuquerque, New Mexico

Sharing encourages caring

When we were first married, my husband Frank's love of football often came between us. I'd never been a fan of the game, but decided I'd better become one, if I wanted to spend any time with him. Frank gladly taught me all about the game and now I'm as big a fan as he is.

Sharing is an important part of our lives. On the flip side, he does things to be with me, when I'm sure he'd rather be doing something else. For instance, he's a great shopper. I have the only husband of all of our friends who will spend all day with me at the malls. He never complains if I drag him to every store in town. That's important to me.

The kids are all grown now and we've retired. We travel a lot and have seen most of the United States. Have you ever been locked in an RV for several months with someone? It makes or breaks you. And talk about sharing. We do just fine and have really grown even closer because of it.

Three years ago we bought a house outside of Quartzsite, Arizona. When we look out the window, our RV is parked right there waiting for our next trip.

We've made great friends here in Arizona. One reason is that we also share much in common. Rock hunting, desert Jeep trips and hiking are among our favorite things to do together and with our friends. We feel so lucky that we both share these interests.

Since we moved to Arizona, Frank has discovered he has short-term memory loss. It's been hard on him and me too. But between all of our great friends and family and the love we have for each other, I know we'll be just fine. We've been married for twenty-three years now, and I'm looking forward to many more, doing what we do best, being together and sharing our lives.

Pat G., Quartzsite, Arizona

You've got Cupid mail

Even before we were married, I was never very good at expressing myself out loud. For a long time my wife Kathy's biggest complaint was that I didn't share my feelings. Then I discovered e-mail and a way to satisfy us both.

I'm a computer programmer and I'm on my computer all day. I'm comfortable with e-mail and at some point began sending Kathy a daily e-love note and it just grew from there. Sometimes it's just a sentence. Sometimes it's a paragraph or to. Sometimes a page.

Last year I saved and printed all 365 of the e-mails I sent her and had them bound at a local copy shop. I titled it "Kathy and Kevin's Book of Love." She no longer complains.

Checking in daily with each other, even if it's by e-mail,

keeps you both on the same page. I thank St. Valentine's for the Internet every day.

Kevin C., Greenbay, Wisconsin

After reading this chapter, test your relationship I.Q. with the **Improve Your Relationship QUIZ BOOK,** *then use the* **Improve Your Relationship WORK BOOK** *to work on the areas of your relationship that need a little help, using the simple action items checklist in the book. Both books are available only by visiting http://www.ImproveYourRelationship.com.*

#20: The Timing / Patience Rule

When it comes to the rhythm method, high-wire trapeze acts and asking for what you want, timing is everything.

How to have a million-dollar relationship

If you've ever watched the popular reality TV show *Survivor*, you know just how important and how difficult it is to be patient, to keep yourself from saying things you shouldn't say or from doing things you shouldn't do.

For most of us, it's nearly impossible.

All the contestants on the show have to do is try to get along with 16 other contestants for 39 days and they have the chance to win one-million dollars. Even with one-million dollars at stake most of them cannot control their emotions. They argue, antagonize, backstab, say the wrong things at the wrong time and generally annoy and alienate their fellow tribe members, knowing full well that what they're doing will likely get them voted off the show at the next opportunity.

The majority of these people, who competed vigorously to be on the show and were chosen over thousands of applicants, are not able to control their emotions for just a few days! Is it any wonder that there are so few happy, long-term relationship survivors.

I've never had a lot of patience and I've always felt I had bad timing, but I realized long ago that it's one of the most important skills to have in a relationship, so I work on it all the time. I may never win one million-dollars, but I've learned how to have a million-dollar relationship.

Shannon S., Detroit, Michigan

You may be dead right, but you'll still be dead

I'll never forget the day my college girlfriend Barbara told me that her father had died. My response was "Thank God, now you can live in peace." I could see immediately from the look on her face that I had said the wrong thing.

In the three years that I had known her she had complained almost daily about her father's drinking, about how he verbally berated her, and how he physically abused her mother. He was an abusive, alcoholic tyrant whom she feared and detested. But he was also her father.

I had forgotten that unspoken rule that you can complain and say anything you want about your family but no matter how horrible they are you don't want to hear someone else saying the same things about them. It was also just bad timing on my part. He had barely been gone a day.

Since that day, many years ago, I've tried to think before I speak. It's a lesson I haven't forgotten. I never saw Barbara again after that day. But I see her horrified expression in my mind every time I'm about to say something that's better left unsaid.

So I guess I have Barbara to thank for my happy relationship today.

Ramon V., St. Louis, Missouri

There's no big secret

Over the years I've learned that if I ask my husband Rashid to do something when he's stressed or busy or preoccupied, I get resistance or it turns into an argument. He's very predictable. If I ask him the same question and he's relaxed or in a receptive mood I usually get what I want.

My problem was that I had lousy timing and didn't know when to ask. My timing was always off. So now, my solution is simply to ask him if he is in the mood or has the time for my question or questions. If he's not, we make an appointment for later in the evening or the next day.

I'm also impatient, so it's difficult for me to wait, but I've learned to be more patient since it improves the chances of getting what I want, without adding stress or transferring my problem to him.

Rachel A., Butte, Montana

It's the first lesson we learn and the first lesson we forget

The first lesson I remember learning as a kid was that if I asked my parents for something at the wrong time I didn't get it. If I had patience and waited for the right moment, I usually got what I wanted. It works the same today with my wife.

It seems so simple yet I hear so many of my buddies complaining that they don't get what they want from their wives and don't think they should have to wait for the right time to ask. My feeling is, if a technique works, why not use it?

Ty A., Tacoma, Washington

The relationship rules of irony

Most people know that if you wait until the end of the year to buy a car, dealers will make great deals because they want to make room for next year's models. Before you ask your boss for a raise you make sure he's in a good mood and not in the middle of a crisis. If you want to earn more money investing in stocks you try to buy low and sell high.

Most of us have learned these basic rules. So why don't we use them in our relationships? The same rules apply because they're common sense.

I think it's because we don't like to think of relationships in practical, non-emotional, non-romantic ways. The irony is, if you're practical and get what you want, you feel and have more time to be more romantic and emotional towards your partner.

Dale E., El Paso, Texas

After reading this chapter, test your relationship I.Q. with the **Improve Your Relationship QUIZ BOOK,** *then use the* **Improve Your Relationship WORK BOOK** *to work on the areas of your relationship that need a little help, using the simple action items checklist in the book. Both books are available only by visiting http://www.ImproveYourRelationship.com.*

#21: The Truthfulness Rule

There are all kinds of lies. Little White lies,
Big Fat lies and Relationship-Buster lies.
The horrible truth is everyone lies.
Choose your lies carefully.

The "Do I look fat in this dress?" lie

Sometimes little white lies are unavoidable and even preferable to the truth. For instance if my wife Zoey asks me if she looks fat in her favorite outfit, or if I find our sexy new neighbor more attractive than her, or if I ever think of anyone else while we're making love, I'd be a fool to be honest. All it would do is hurt her. And since none of those things are important to me, why would I want to threaten our marriage and open up a can of worms?

On the other hand, on issues that really matter, not telling the truth can be even more harmful to a relationship. I think the secret to a happy marriage is in knowing when to be honest and when to spare your partner's feelings. It's not always easy to know when to do which.

My rule of thumb, to help me determine which, is to ask myself if I'm telling my wife the truth to make *me* feel better (for instance to ease my guilty conscience). If I am then it's probably going to hurt her and not be helpful to either of us.

On the other hand, if it's something that would hurt Zoey if she didn't know, I know I need to be honest and tell her, no matter how difficult it is for me.

Gabriel T., Reno, Nevada

Can you handle the truth?

When it comes to telling the truth, I always remember Jack Nicholson in the movie *A Few Good Men*, when he says "You can't handle the truth!"

I always imagine he's talking about me. My first marriage was a lie, because I didn't want to know the truth. I guess I knew all along that my husband was having an affair but I didn't ask or confront him because I didn't really want to know. I was afraid our marriage would be over. By ignoring the situation it only got worse and he eventually left me anyway. I learned the hard way.

Before marrying my present husband Zack, we talked a lot about being open and honest. We agreed to always be honest with one another. Even if it's painful. Because we're honest, I believe there's no problem that we can't solve or overcome and that's a liberating feeling.

Before I could be honest with another person I had to start being honest with myself. I believe this is a major key to a happy relationship.

Heather G., Des Moines, Iowa

Don't keep the truth in the closet, or your partner in the dark

Honesty and trust was very difficult for my partner John and I in the beginning. But after a couple of years, after we both had opportunities to screw up big time and were honest about it, we learned to trust each other.

This doesn't mean we have to tell each other every transgression, mistake or breach of agreement. Some seem to be, and are, insignificant at the time they happen. Some grow into more than you expect. When that happens we either bring up the subject and confess, or if the other finds out and asks about it, we don't deny it.

It's like coming out of the closet: the truth works wonders.
Bill D., Seattle, Washington

After reading this chapter, test your relationship I.Q. with the **Improve Your Relationship QUIZ BOOK,** *then use the* **Improve Your Relationship WORK BOOK** *to work on the areas of your relationship that need a little help, using the simple action items checklist in the book. Both books are available only by visiting http://www.ImproveYourRelationship.com.*

Section 5
The Teamwork Challenge

Follow these eight simple rules if you want
to be Relationship Champions

#22: The Cheerleading Rule

Treat your partner like the most important person in the world and you'll become the most important person in the world to your partner.

Do a few back flips for your team

We all need someone who will root for us, no matter what. We all want someone who's always on our side cheering us on, someone who believes in and encourages us to do our best.

My cheerleader is my husband Dimitri. He makes it exciting to play for him. I want to do my best, knowing he's on the sidelines watching. But I also know that even if I fail, he'll still be there to encourage me over the next hurdle and the one after that.

Dimitri has inspired me to be a cheerleader, as well. I never went out to for the cheerleading team in high school but here I am in middle-age eagerly doing the splits for our winning team.

Sonya V., Fort Worth, Texas

Don't forget whose team you're on

My girlfriends and I used to get together for lunch every week and the conversation invariably revolved around our disappointment with our husbands. Our rotten, or absent or abusive husbands were always the center of our conversation.

One day I realized that putting-down, complaining about, and trashing my partner was a bad reflection on me. If he was so horrible and I stayed with him, or didn't share my frustrations with him, what did this say about me? I asked myself one day would we ever talk this way about our children?

We defend our kids, give them unconditional love, support them, cheer them on even when we secretly know they have no chance of winning. So why don't we do the same with our spouses?

I lost my appetite for dishing the dirt with the girls after that. Instead, these days I meet my husband for lunch once a week. If we have any complaints, we discuss them over a Happy Meal, just to remind us which team we're on.

Suzanne E., Boise, Idaho

Are you flirting with disaster?

We were very young when we married and a bit immature. My husband Andrew had always been a big flirt but I assumed his flirting days would be over once we said "I do." But old habits die hard.

At first I was angry and hurt and felt disrespected. My first impulse was to flirt with other men and to hurt him back. The problem with this plan was that I loved him and didn't want to hurt him. So I tried another tactic. I tried reverse psychology and did just the opposite of what I wanted to do.

The next time we were in public and he flirted with a woman in front of me, I calmly said "You can flirt with her, but the only one I want to flirt with is you—you're the only guy in this place I would give a second look to."

Making him feel special, like he was the most important guy in the room, not only made him feel wonderful but he also felt a bit of guilt and shame for not treating me with the same respect or admiration. It helped that what I said was true, but even if it weren't true it was much more effective in getting what I wanted than if I had complained or nagged or threatened him.

Now, the only flirting he does in public is with me. At least when we're together and that's all that really matters. We're on the same team now. He knows I'm rooting for him and for us and that makes him want to do the same.

Michele M., Palm Springs, California

After reading this chapter, test your relationship I.Q. with the **Improve Your Relationship QUIZ BOOK,** *then use the* **Improve Your Relationship WORK BOOK** *to work on the areas of your relationship that need a little help, using the simple action items checklist in the book. Both books are available only by visiting http://www.ImproveYourRelationship.com.*

#23: The Dependence Rule

Too much time together can be smothering.
Too little time together can cause you to drift apart.
Like the Three Bears, keep exploring until you
discover a balance that's just right.

Are you getting too much of a good thing?

When we were first dating, I loved it that Jan wanted to be with me all the time, and seemed to like to do all the things that I like to do. My previous girlfriend was just the opposite.

After we married, what seemed to be a plus while dating, turned into a minus. While I may have enjoyed all the attention and time in the beginning, Jan's clingy, needy behavior began to feel smothering. For example, she would call me at least five times a day at work just to check in. I didn't have any alone time and I began to see her as insecure and someone who didn't have a life of her own.

When I first brought it up to her she felt rejected and hurt. She said that her way of showing me her love was to spend time with me. I tried to explain that I enjoyed our time together but needed some time alone as well; time that didn't have anything to do with her. But the more I pulled away the tighter she held on. I tried everything but nothing seemed to get through to her.

At my wits end, I considered separating and even thought about divorce, but I loved her and wanted to make the marriage work, so I hung in there. When all else failed, I asked her to help me figure out how to get the space I needed.

Asking Jan for her help in coming up with a solution shifted the power back to me. By holding on so tight she maintained the power. She could veto every suggestion I made or every attempt I made to change things. By asking her to come up with a solution, I was in control again. Yet so was she, so we both won.

Having Jan come up with the solution turned our relationship around almost overnight. Suddenly, she was able to see the problem from a different point of view. Since the changes we made were her ideas, she was also glad to make them.

Now, whenever one of us has a problem, we ask the other for help in solving it. It's empowering for both of us. This has been our secret to a happy—and independent—relationship.

Kirk L., Winston-Salem, North Carolina

Take an interest in your partner's interests

Robert and I just celebrated our 39th wedding anniversary. We've had many ups and downs, from health problems to financial problems, yet we're still together and in love. One reason is that we share each other's interests.

Robert loves history and reenacts in the American Civil War and American Revolution. Many other husbands in these groups go alone to events because their wives don't share their interest. I go with my husband. I have outfits to dress in the time period. It isn't something I'd do on my own, but I do it for him. Instead of spending the day apart or arguing because he's leaving me for the day, we're together. We've made new friends through these groups, and enjoy our time together.

In return, Robert knows I love crafts and we go to craft shows and craft shops together. He shares my interest by encouraging my activities and providing a place in our home for my crafts.

Taking an interest in your partner's interests, keeps your partner interested in you.

Bea S., Manchester, Connecticut

Like a telephone, it works both ways

There are certain social events that John, my partner of 30 years, refuses to go to, and I absolutely refuse to miss. That's fine, we don't have to do everything together. But there are certain things that I absolutely INSIST that he does with me. He knows that there's no getting around it and I know that he hates it. Tough! You do it, you get through it, you come home and it's over with. It works the other way around too.

Bill D., Seattle, Washington

After reading this chapter, test your relationship I.Q. with the **Improve Your Relationship QUIZ BOOK,** *then use the* **Improve Your Relationship WORK BOOK** *to work on the areas of your relationship that need a little help, using the simple action items checklist in the book. Both books are available only by visiting http://www.ImproveYourRelationship.com.*

#24: The Independence Rule

Give each other space to grow and to discover
new gifts to bring back to the relationship.
Remember the saying—absence makes
the heart grow fonder.

Make time for private time

After eight very happy years together, we've found that
one of the keys to success is to keep private space for ourselves in our home.

We each have our own office space where we can work,
read, or contemplate things in private when we choose. We
also have separate bathing facilities so we don't get in each
other's way when preparing to leave the house.

Sometimes simple things work the best.

Sidelia R., Oxford, Ohio

Your partner's hobby means time for you

When we were first married, I was always irritated because my husband Greg spent every free moment in front of
the TV, watching sports. After years of resentment and
nagging, I finally realized that this was not a game I was
going to win.

The time we did spend together was loving and caring,
but I wanted more. I finally gave up and found a hobby of
my own. I discovered a passion and talent for quilting.

Today I'm grateful that I have the time and space to
pursue my own interests. I now look at this free time as a gift,

where I once looked at as not being loved.
Ali P., Tulsa, Oklahoma

Support your partner's desire for independence and your partner will find you more desirable

Kevin and I have been together for almost five years, and are expecting our first baby in January. Kevin is a writer.

At times, especially when I've gone through sad times, I've been tempted to distract him from his writing to get him to spend time with me. It took some time for me to realize that by giving him his space for writing, I was showing him how much I love him.

We often refer to being supportive in this way as "being on the team," even though we're not sports people. I'll get on Kevin's Writing Team by helping him to submit short stories for publication, and he gets on Rosalie's Spirituality Team by going with me to religious services.

What we've realized is that we don't have to do everything together, or be interested in all the same things—as long as we can actively support those things that are most important to one another.
Rosalie R., Urbana, Illinois

Don't lose yourself in your relationship

One of the "secrets" of our happy marriage was given to me by my husband Larry, shortly after we were married. He told me that I was spending too much time on him, doing things for him, thinking too much about him.

He said that he loved me, that he fell in love with me and that he didn't want me to forget me. He explained the importance of remaining an individual and seeking out my own interests. He didn't want me to lose my sense of self.

Larry has always been supportive in whatever I wanted

to do, and I've always supported him as well. He says, "We are two that make one, the strength of two makes a powerful one." This statement has been proven over and over throughout the years.

Amy C., Prescott, Arizona

After reading this chapter, test your relationship I.Q. with the **Improve Your Relationship QUIZ BOOK,** *then use the* **Improve Your Relationship WORK BOOK** *to work on the areas of your relationship that need a little help, using the simple action items checklist in the book. Both books are available only by visiting http://www.ImproveYourRelationship.com.*

#25: The Leadership Rule

A relationship is a dance and only one of you can lead at a time. Don't compete with each other or you'll trip. Decide who's best at the Tango and who's best at the Twist, and take turns.

Who's the boss?

When my best friend Tanya married her husband, all of her friends knew it wouldn't last and wondered why she couldn't see it.

Tanya is a lovable, but high-maintenance woman. She's opinionated, assertive and domineering. And those are her better qualities. The man she married had the exact same personality. Talk about adding fuel to the fire. They both wanted to run the relationship—to be in charge—and they clashed on every issue.

I'm also a strong person and I like other strong personalities. I lose my patience with milquetoast types. Like Tanya, I also married someone like myself. The difference is that my husband Stephen and I take turns being in charge. If it's an area we both feel passionate about, we just draw straws.

For instance when it comes to food—preparation, selection, whether to dine in or out—we're both very opinionated. When it comes to planning social events, vacations and most other activities, Stephen usually takes care of everything. When it comes to finances, paying the bills, investing and that sort of thing, I'm in charge.

It's sometimes a challenge to divide up the things we both like to do and the things neither of us likes to do, but it's always worth the effort. And instead of spending time arguing, we spend our time eating and partying.

Natasha A., San Francisco, California

Too many cooks can spoil the meal

Both my husband Robert and I both enjoy cooking, so we take turns. This sounds ordinary but many couples today eat out, or bring food in from fast-food restaurants.

I understand we live in a busy society, but one or two nights a week have dinner at home with food you or your spouse has cooked. Each week we have a complete meal at the table. We unplug the telephone so we can eat and talk undisturbed. It's one of our special times together.

Bea S., Manchester, Connecticut

Don't be stubborn—ask someone who knows, for directions

Why is it that we would rather ask a bartender for advice on relationships than ask someone who already has a happy relationship? Why do we drive around in circles for hours, without stopping to ask for a map or for directions from someone who knows? Stubbornness? Ego? Pride?

If your relationship isn't going the way you want it to, or isn't turning out the way you planned, stop and ask for help. Start by asking your partner for help. Your partner may not even know you're lost. But, since nearly everyone is willing to help someone in need, it can really turn things around.

If your partner isn't able to help, and the two of you can't find a happy couple to ask for their advice, then find a good therapist. Whatever you do, stop and ask someone for help.

If your relationship isn't working, one of you has to take the lead. Don't waste any more time driving down dead end roads. There are plenty of relationship road maps available.

My husband Shaun has never been too proud to ask for help. He's a true leader, with the strength of character to know when to follow. And in this area, I've followed his lead and because of it our relationship has never taken a wrong turn.

Kit R., Madison, Wisconsin

Liberate yourself from other people's expectations

I love feeling taken care of and protected by my partner Luke. I love staying at home with our children and I'm happy to let him make most of the important decisions in our relationship.

I know it's not politically correct or very liberated, and many of my friends think I'm being taken advantage of, but I don't. Not every relationship has to be created equal. If you're both getting what you want, how can that be wrong?

Luke is an old-fashioned guy with old-fashioned values and I find that comforting. It's not that I couldn't make the decisions and take charge if I needed to. I just don't feel a need to compete.

If you're both happy with your rules, however unequal they may seem to others, you can have a happy relationship. We have, for 11 years.

Carrie R., Jackson, Mississippi

After reading this chapter, test your relationship I.Q. with the **Improve Your Relationship QUIZ BOOK,** *then use the* **Improve Your Relationship WORK BOOK** *to work on the areas of your relationship that need a little help, using the simple action items checklist in the book. Both books are available only by visiting http://www.ImproveYourRelationship.com.*

#26: The Reliability Rule

If your partner packed your parachute
would you jump out of a plane? If you want
your mate to be there for you, make sure
you're someone worth being there for.

**From the most unassuming to the most impressive home,
every house needs a solid foundation**

For me, being able to rely on my wife makes all the difference in the world. No matter what happens in our lives I know I can always depend on her. When I'm down, I always depend on her to cheer me up. When I'm stressed, she knows just what to say and do to help me relax. She makes me want to do the same for her.

I don't think we give people enough credit for being there for us. I credit her rock-solid reliability for providing the foundation for our happy nine-year relationship. It doesn't hurt that she's sexy too.

Campbell R., Minneapolis, Minnesota

Predictable can be boring but reliable can be freeing

When you're driving down a lonely highway in the middle of nowhere on a stormy night, would you rather be driving a flashy convertible or a rugged, all-terrain, four-wheel drive?

My first husband Joe was a flashy convertible. We certainly had lots of flash and fun, but our relationship skidded off the highway at the first sign of gathering clouds.

Mike, my husband of the past six years, is in it for the long haul. I know I can count on him in any kind of relationship weather and he makes me want to be there for him in return. We regularly check the pressure in the tires and make sure our battery is charged. Neither of us wants to get stranded on a lonely road one night all alone.

Reliability is one of the keys to going the distance in a relationship. I look forward to the long road ahead together.

Carmen M., Youngstown, Pennsylvania

Nine times out of ten, being specific will get to what you want — you can count on it

What do you rely on your partner for? For companionship, sexual relief, affection and intimacy, emotional support, financial support?

When you want something from someone it always helps if you're specific. For example, if your partner is unreliable and it's causing a problem, it won't help if you say, "I can never count on you." When you accuse and criticize, your partner will be even less willing to give you what you want.

Instead, be specific and ask for help. For instance, if you need your partner to be more financially reliable, you might say "By the time we pay all our bills our current income isn't enough to put anything away for our retirement, which worries me. Can you help me figure out a way to do both?" This question starts a dialogue; the first statement starts a fight and stops any dialogue.

I mention reliability because my husband Ted and I struggled with this for years before I became clear about what I wanted. It took me a long time to realize that I was never going to get what I wanted by accusing and insulting him. The technique I discovered worked for us. Ted's now one of the most reliable people I know. To my surprise I also discovered that this technique works for most other areas of difficulty in a relationship, as well.

Getting clear about what you want from your partner and being specific about what you ask for, has been a major key to happiness in our relationship.
Christine H., San Diego, California

After reading this chapter, test your relationship I.Q. with the **Improve Your Relationship QUIZ BOOK,** *then use the* **Improve Your Relationship WORK BOOK** *to work on the areas of your relationship that need a little help, using the simple action items checklist in the book. Both books are available only by visiting http://www.ImproveYourRelationship.com.*

#27: The Responsibility Rule

Take 100% responsibility for making your
relationship work and your partner will likely
want to give 100% back—with interest.
The key is being the first to give it.

Use your refrigerator to win the blame game

For years my wife and I played the blame game. I blamed
her for not paying the bills on time and one-hundred or more
other infractions. She blamed me for not getting the kids to
school on time and at least one-hundred other misdeeds.

Finally, we had enough and just sat down and made a very
long list of things that needed to be done. We then divided the
list up between us. We put it on the refrigerator to remind us
who's responsible for what. We no longer need to play the
blame game. Now everyone knows who's responsible for
what.

Sometimes I think we just overlook the obvious and needlessly complicate our lives. Knowing who's responsible also
makes it easier to be responsible.

Tyrell J., Mobile, Alabama

Sometimes you have to give up the battle to win the war

The hardest part about being in a relationship, for me
anyway, was being responsible and taking responsibility for
my actions.

You have to be responsible at work, you have to be a responsible driver and you have to be a responsible parent. It

often feels like a conspiracy to make you grow up. I wanted my relationship to be fun and passionate and spontaneous. The last thing I wanted it to be was responsible. But by being irresponsible, my wife Ting Ting and I spent so much of our time together fighting that there wasn't time left for fun, passion and spontaneity.

It took me some time but I learned that these things were only possible if I were dependable and responsible. Okay, so I may be a "responsible adult" today but I'm having more fun now than I did as a kid. Sometimes you just have to stop fighting it.

Ian B., Cincinnati, Ohio

Take responsibility for your partner's feelings and it will change the way *you* act

I know that we're responsible for our own reactions and that no one else can make us feel or do something we don't want to. But I still can't help feeling responsible when I do something that hurts my wife's feelings. Not wanting to hurt her in any way has helped me in our relationship. It's made it easy to be responsible for my actions and to make every effort to not do anything that would ever hurt her. And she does the same for me. It may be simple but it's worked for us.

Lyle G., Louisville, Kentucky

There's never a good excuse for a bad relationship

A good friend of mine complains often that her relationships never seem to work out. She's attractive, warm, caring, has a college degree and a job she loves. But when it comes to intimate relationships she doesn't have a clue. She always has an excuse to explain why it's not her fault that they don't work out.

When she lived in San Francisco, her excuse was that all

the men in the city were either gay or afraid of commitment. When she moved to New York, her excuse was that all the men were Italian "Guidos," and "everyone knows" that Italians don't respect women. When I offer that there must be a few non-Italians in Manhattan, she concedes, but then explains why none of them are relationship material either.

The Jewish men are all mama's boys or selfish, the doctors and lawyers are all married and only looking for a mistress, the blue-collar workers are just looking for mothers to care for them and to have their babies, and on and on.

Sometimes I laugh to myself, wondering if she really believes her own excuses, or if she believes anyone else takes what she says seriously. Until she's ready to give up her rigid beliefs and expectations and to stop discriminating against all possible relationship candidates, my friend will remain single.

My friend needs to take some responsibility for being alone. If every Jewish man, every doctor, every bus driver and every Italian lived up to their stereotypes she might be credible, but obviously reality and my friend do not see eye to eye.

Taking the responsibility for who you choose to have a relationship with and for doing everything you can to make it work, is very powerful.

My husband Warren and I both take responsibility for doing whatever we have to do to have a good relationship. We start by overcoming our prejudices about each other, along with our rigid beliefs that get in the way of our goal.

I've shared our secret with my friend but she can think of lots of reasons why doing what we do won't work for her.

Maddie S., Mexico City, Mexico

Taking responsibility is sexy

One of the things I love about my husband Anthony is that he always takes responsibility for anything he's done wrong. He never tries to shift the blame or pass the buck and I find

that very sexy and appealing. It's also inspiring and makes me want to be a better, more responsible person. It's lots of small things like this that have helped us have a happy relationship for nine years now.
Lucinda L., Portland, Oregon

After reading this chapter, test your relationship I.Q. with the **Improve Your Relationship QUIZ BOOK,** *then use the* **Improve Your Relationship WORK BOOK** *to work on the areas of your relationship that need a little help, using the simple action items checklist in the book. Both books are available only by visiting http://www.ImproveYourRelationship.com.*

#28: The Sacrifice Rule

In the Love Olympics, when you sacrifice
yourself for the team you can still win the gold.

**To borrow from an old saying, winning couples never
quit and quitting couples never win**

Sometimes struggling together can make your relationship
stronger. Don't leave when it gets difficult or when your mate
needs you the most.

My boyfriend and I have been together for five years and
have not had the easiest time financially. I was out of work and
he scraped pennies and his small government check for us to
make our rent. Then he was out of work for a while and I
supported him. It wasn't easy on either of us. But we held on
to each other and didn't leave and it made our bond stronger.
Freda N., Memphis, Tennessee

Are you placing a winning or losing bet?

Life is full of sacrifices, both large and small. We give up a
certain amount of freedom to be in a relationship. We give up
even more freedom to have and care for our kids. But these are
sacrifices that return more to us in the end. They're short-term
sacrifices. All they require is maturity, and a bit of delayed
gratification. I call these the winning sacrifices.

The losing sacrifices are when you give up your dignity or
when you sacrifice someone else to save yourself. I believe the

key to a happy relationship is being able to distinguish between the two.

Conrad T., Atlanta, Georgia

It's not about *you* anymore, it's about the two of you for evermore

After 28 years of marriage, my husband left me. I was single for a year and then remarried. Before I remarried, I thought about all the mistakes I made during the first marriage and will make sure they don't happen again. I now know what a happy marriage is and how to keep it happy.

The key to a happy marriage is total, complete unselfishness. You must put your husband's wishes or your wife's wishes before your own. You must put their feelings first, and not worry about how YOU feel. It's the only way. By doing so, you'll find that things you really want you'll get because of the love you have and the sacrifices you've make for your spouse.

When a problem comes along in our home, I now think before I react. I say to myself, "what will make him the happiest?" I don't ask what it is that *I* want, but what will make him happy.

Always put your spouse first, above your work, your family, your hobbies, sports or whatever. Your partner's feelings are the most important thing to you. TV is just TV. Sports are just sports. If he wants to eat out at a certain place and you want to go to another, go to his place. He'll likely want to take you to your place next time.

By putting my needs second, after his, my husband, in turn, *wants* to put my needs first, in front of his, so we both effortlessly get what we want anyway.

I've discovered it's easy to be married if you aren't selfish and if you just follow this one rule. Love begets love. Sacrifice begets sacrifice. Whatever you do for your partner, your partner will see your example and return it.

It works like magic.
Margo F., Tucker, Georgia

After reading this chapter, test your relationship I.Q. with the **Improve Your Relationship QUIZ BOOK,** *then use the* **Improve Your Relationship WORK BOOK** *to work on the areas of your relationship that need a little help, using the simple action items checklist in the book. Both books are available only by visiting http://www.ImproveYourRelationship.com.*

#29: The Support Rule

In relationships, as in basketball, if you don't have the support of your team, you'll be benched and never make MVP (Most Valuable Partner).

Would you go around the world for your first mate ?

The number one characteristic I looked for in a woman when I was considering marriage was how supportive she would be.

My mother spent her married life belittling and tearing down my father. He finally had enough and left us. I was determined that I would not to marry a woman like my mother, no matter what I had to do.

Before I proposed to Sarah I told her that if we were married I wanted to quit my job and spend a year or two together sailing around the world. I knew she suffered from sea sickness, when I said this. Without hesitation she said she thought it would be a wonderful adventure.

I never intended to quit my job. It was just a test and she passed it with flying colors. Maybe it was unkind to test her in this way, but I had to know and hoped that she would understand my reasons for doing it. We did spend our honeymoon on my boat, but we never made it out of the harbor.

Our marriage has been smooth sailing from the start and I believe it's because we support each other. Before you set sail, I recommend that you truly know your first mate.

Bobby K., Marina Del Rey, California

You don't always get what you want, but as the song goes, you usually get what you need

Growing up, I was put-down by my father for just about everything. Nothing I ever did was good enough for him. I didn't realize it at that time but he was a frightened and insecure man who never thought *he* was good enough and projected it onto me.

I didn't see it until we had been together for some time but Randy, the man I married, was really my dad in disguise.

Not long after the honeymoon I was laid off from my job as a caterer for a large restaurant. For years, in the back of my mind, I had fantasized about starting my own catering business. This seemed like the right opportunity. Randy, however, was not at all supportive of my new venture.

Sure, money would be tight, but that wasn't really the issue. We planned to have children, but not for a few years, so it seemed to me to be the ideal time. He was reluctant at first to discuss his misgivings but eventually revealed that his mother had always put him down and discouraged him from doing anything creative or impractical. He wanted to be an artist but instead became a bookkeeper. Part of his lack of support was a result of envy. Partly it was fear and partly he was just repeating what he had been taught.

I don't think Randy will ever be able to express excitement for what I'm doing. I would love it if he were able to be emotionally supportive, but that's not who he is. But he does support me in the way he knows how. He does the books for my new catering business, which means the world to me.

So, as the song goes, you don't always get what you want, but you do usually get what you need. And I've discovered, to my surprise, that if you're not greedy, that it's usually more than enough.

Liddia G., Charleston, South Carolina

Good girls and boys sometimes make bad partners

Kelly's parents never approved of me. Kelly was my first wife. I didn't have the right job, didn't make enough money, wasn't ambitious enough and didn't spend enough time with our daughter.

Their list of complaints was endless and very creative. It didn't bother me what they thought. What bothered me was that Kelly needed to be her parent's good girl more than she needed to be a good wife. She never really supported me. She never took my side. She never stood up to her folks. Year after year she allowed them to drive a wedge between us and eventually it drove us apart.

I learned my lesson and am now married to a woman who puts her husband and her family before her parents, before her job and before all the petty, everyday challenges that can threaten a relationship. I learned the hard way that a partner's support is stronger than all love in the world.

In many ways I still love Kelly but it just wasn't enough to keep us together.

Tre R., Kansas City, Missouri

To have a dream relationship, help your partner realize his or her crazy, kooky and farfetched dreams

If I could give just one piece of advice to couples it's this: encourage each other's crazy dreams, no matter how kooky, farfetched or just plain stupid they may seem to you.

When my husband announced he was dropping out of computer training to get a degree in music, I actually broke down and cried. "Music?! What on earth can you do with a music degree?! We're gonna be broke forever!" I thought. Though I had many misgivings, I agreed to support and encourage him while he pursued his passion for music.

Though he just started classes a few months ago, the

change in him has been dramatic. He's happier, more driven and more energetic than I've ever seen him—all because he's pursuing his own path, not the path that others tell him to be on.

I've learned to relax and let the future take care of itself. Who am I to say music isn't the right career path for him, or to assume he won't make money at it?

People don't quit dreaming simply because they get married. Yet some people think that the impetuous, free spirit they fell in love with is supposed to magically morph into a dutiful, mortgage-paying, corporate slug, simply out of obligation. To have a happy relationship, both of you must be allowed to pursue your dreams!

Erin K., Denver, Colorado

After reading this chapter, test your relationship I.Q. with the **Improve Your Relationship QUIZ BOOK,** *then use the* **Improve Your Relationship WORK BOOK** *to work on the areas of your relationship that need a little help, using the simple action items checklist in the book. Both books are available only by visiting http://www.ImproveYourRelationship.com.*

Section 6
The Obstacles Challenge

Follow these nine simple rules if you want
to build Relationship Muscle

#30: The Abuse / Addiction Rule

You can argue all you want with the referee and judges, but you'll still be benched or kicked off the team for abusive behavior. Anger and hostility is never a winning strategy.

When it comes to abuse, physical or verbal—one strike and you're out

In 1983 I escaped from an abusive relationship. I moved from Germany to the U.S. shortly after, where I met Steve. To make a long story short, we ended up getting married in late 1984. When I met Steve, I was a wreck. A year of violent domestic abuse had left me battered inside and out. Steve was so caring and sensitive and listened so attentively to my soap opera life stories.

Sometimes I wondered what he saw in me. Only much later did I realize that his self-esteem was so low, that I was perfect for him. I made him feel good by comparison. I began to realize that he didn't love the real me, who slowly emerged and blossomed under his initial care. When I grew too strong, he turned violent in an attempt to hold me down. He couldn't be a knight without a damsel in distress and so he turned into a knight-mare.

The first few years it was mostly verbal abuse; eventually he became physical. I managed to do the right thing this time: I pressed charges. Subsequently we went through years of extreme post-divorce hostility. We even had a court order to exchange the kids at the police station!

During our courtship there were many red flags that I

should have seen, but I didn't want to believe that this could happen to me again. It looks as if I may never get the proper ending I still hope for. I picture it in the form of an apology. I realize now, it may never come. The important thing is that I got out and I made it. And my eyes are now open to red flags.

By the way, I'm married again, with another child. This time I went in with my eyes open.

Heide A.W. K., Tecumseh, Michigan

If the Jerry Springer show calls—hang up!

After years of being used, abused and taken advantage of by men, I decided that my life was starting to resemble an episode of *Jerry Springer*. I couldn't allow it to go on any longer.

I remembered that at one point I had been a strong woman. I needed to figure out where I'd gone wrong. Exactly when did my life start to spiral down into a world of yelling, crying and arguing? Why was I taking care of a man who was best friends with a bottle named Jack, and our toilet seat— after he and Jack had gone too far?

One day I just looked myself right in the mirror, however lame that may sound, and screamed, "WAKE UP!" Then I packed up my stuff and left his ass to fend for himself. And I didn't go back. Sure there where plenty of times when I missed the feeling of him lying next to me. There were also nights he would call and plead with me to come over, but I held firm. I kept my panties on and found other ways to occupy my time.

Hey, if you miss the orgasms, trust me, there are plenty of ways to fix that little problem and men don't even have to be part of the picture. I've had plenty of nights of ecstasy involving me, myself and I and no sweaty man to deal with after the fact. I'm not saying to lock yourself in your room and have fun alone forever, but just don't depend on a man to make you happy.

I started to feel adequate when I realized that in order to be in a place where I was one-hundred percent content I had to make myself feel good first.You are your own best medicine. You and only you know what's good for you. So go out and do it and do it alone first. Then you can find someone who will respect you for the strong woman that you are and not step on you and discard you like trash. Oh, and invest in a toy. Men have their little toys why can't we have ours.

Sabrina R., the Internet

Surprise! He's not the problem

If, after bargaining, bribing and threatening your abusive or addicted partner, he or she refuses to seek counseling, cut your losses and get out fast.

If you leave, you won't improve your relationship with your partner but you will improve your relationship with yourself. I know, I was in an abusive relationship for years.

Once I got the courage, I left, sought counseling for myself and my life improved dramatically. I learned how to be in a healthy relationship with myself.

I always thought he was the problem. But it was all about me. I was the one who stayed in an abusive relationship. Only after discovering this was I able to meet the man of my dreams. We've been together for 16 happy years now.

Dominique I., Duluth, Minnesota

If your partner is abusive you don't have a relationship, you have a situation

Abuse is to a relationship what rape is to sex. It's all about the violence; it's not about sex and certainly not about love. In other words, you can't improve something you don't have. I don't believe abusers ever completely stop abusing. They may learn how to control themselves better, they may learn better behavioral skills, but they rarely change their core personality.

If you're living with an abuser you can either resign yourself to it or leave and improve yourself. I chose to leave and only then was I able to meet a wonderful man to spend my life with.

Jennifer J., Spokane, Washington

After reading this chapter, test your relationship I.Q. with the **Improve Your Relationship QUIZ BOOK,** *then use the* **Improve Your Relationship WORK BOOK** *to improve the areas of your relationship that need a little help, using the simple action items checklist. Both books are available only by visiting http://www.ImproveYourRelationship.com.*

#31: The Change Rule

Unless you're writing a country song and need a little heartache and inspiration, don't try to change your partner. At the same time, expect your partner to change in ways you didn't expect.

Don't get trapped in a time warp or your relationship may get sucked into a black hole

What's important to you when you're 18 or 20, usually isn't important at all when you're 35 or 40. People evolve. Their interests, values, personalities change. Some people change more than others. I've grown considerably as a person from who I was when I was 18 and met my ex-husband.

He, on the other hand, really hasn't changed much at all. He lives like it's still the 1970s. For him he's still content if he has pot, beer and a hunting license. If one partner changes and the other doesn't, or if both change and grow in different directions, their relationship is at risk.

Growing together is the key, but it takes effort and desire from *both* of you.

Joy B., Kansas City, Missouri

Your relationship can still be a holiday—even if you no longer get a card

Thirty years ago, when we first got together, John and I used to do all the cooking together. Now he does all of the cooking. It's no longer something we share. This seems to have worked out okay for us, but it isn't what I expected at the beginning of the relationship.

I also used to send holiday cards to friends and family that we hadn't heard from in the last year. I'd enclose a note to each. Now I keep track of who sends one year and I reciprocate the following year (elderly aunts and uncles who have trouble writing are the only exception, they get one anyway). I feel certain that this more selective, less open style of annual communication bothers John. I think that he would like me to be more inclusive like I was in former years, but I'm not and he accepts it. So in that little sense, I'm not the same person I was when we met.

People change. You've got to expect them to. And they don't always change in the manner or direction you want them to. Accept them for who they become. Just like your children, if you have any, you have certain expectations, but they have their own lives and seldom turn out exactly, often not even close to, the way you want.

Bill D., Seattle, Washington

Schedule a regular relationship check-up

Just because you have a happy relationship today doesn't mean you and your partner will be happy tomorrow. Things can change. There's no finish line. Kids come along. Jobs change. We develop new interests. Outside pressures impact on us. I found it's important to check in with my partner regularly.

We schedule regular relationship check-ups. Prevention is less painful than waiting until you have a major malfunction—whether it's car maintenance or health care.

My wife Molly and I use a calendar. We schedule a weekend away each month to talk about us and where we are with each other and our lives. She's a party planner and I'm a mechanic, so you could say it just comes naturally to us.

Travis D., San Antonio, Texas

Make it your problem to help solve your partner's problem

Over the years I think I've read every self-help relationship book on the shelves. They all seem to agree that if you're going to make a change in your relationship you have to start with yourself and just make a decision to do it. It's a choice. It's up to you. They rarely mention, though, how difficult it is sometimes to make that choice.

It seems so much easier to change someone else than to change ourselves. After all they're the one with the problem, so why can't they just take our word for it and change? The truth is, we may have just as many problems as our partner, it's just more difficult, if not impossible, to recognize them. So we just keep blindly focusing on theirs.

Since I can't see my problems and my partner's are in my face, I still focus on "his" problems, but now, instead of trying to get him to change or to solve his own problems, I take responsibility for solving his problems.

For instance, my husband Grant doesn't fight fair. He lashes out when he's angry and then leaves the room, not allowing me to respond. Instead of escalating the situation as I used to do, since I know I can't get him to change (I've tried, believe me) I've changed the way *I* respond. Instead of lashing out at him in return I now remain calm and wait for the storm to settle. When he cools off and is ready to discuss the problem, I bring it up. I just ignore the angry things he says that camouflage the main issue and just keep focused on finding a solution to the problem at hand.

He's not the most mature guy in the world when it comes to fighting fairly but I know that. So for me to keep complaining about reality would be just as immature. If solving a problem means I have to be the mature one then that's okay with me.

I've discovered it's so much easier to change how *you*

respond to "your partner's problem" than it is to try to change your partner. For me this has been the key.

Tricia P., London, England

After reading this chapter, test your relationship I.Q. with the **Improve Your Relationship QUIZ BOOK,** *then use the* **Improve Your Relationship WORK BOOK** *to work on the areas of your relationship that need a little help, using the simple action items checklist in the book. Both books are available only by visiting http://www.ImproveYourRelationship.com.*

#32: The Compromise Rule

Half a cookie, half a million dollars and half a day at the beach are still pretty good deals. Half a movie, half a sentence and half an orgasm are worse than none at all. Make sure both of you win at least half of something *worth* having or you'll compromise your relationship.

Don't give up something more important for something less important

I remember complaining, a while back, to a single friend of mine, that I've always wanted to build my dream house in the desert. Unfortunately, my partner of six years can't take the heat and prefers a colder, mountainous climate. My friend said that there is nothing more important than our dreams and that I should follow my dream and build my house anyway.

I thought about it for a moment and replied that my dream house wouldn't be a dream house if I had to spend my nights there without my wife. Sharing it with a partner was part of the dream.

My partner and I have decided to compromise and move near the coast. There's lots of sand for me, as well as a nice cool sea breeze for her. My friend has chosen to remain single and is living in her dream house, alone.

Chandler H., Tampa, Florida

Make him a deal he can't refuse

How do you get your partner to compromise if he or she doesn't want to? This was a question I asked for many years before I found an answer.

My husband Rob was a bachelor for many years before we married and was used to doing what he wanted, when he wanted and to getting what he wanted when he wanted. He wasn't used to compromising. To get him to compromise took some work. I did it by discovering what's important to him, which then gave me a bargaining chip and some leverage.

If your partner has something you want, find out what you have that he wants and then negotiate or make a deal. For instance, Rob loves to attend sports events on the weekends (and there seems to be one event or another nearly every weekend of the year). I prefer to go out to dinner or a movie on the weekends. During the week, he prefers to stay in.

We tried alternating every other weekend but he wasn't really getting what he wanted. I tried attending his events with him but then I wasn't getting what I wanted.

Our compromise was for him to choose the activities during the weekends—Saturday and Sunday—and for me to choose during the week, including Fridays. He's willing to go out to dinner at least once a week in order to have his weekends free. I can live with dinner and a movie one night during the week and on Friday nights. And I've come to enjoy having my weekends free, so it works for both of us.

Compromise takes effort, but it sure beats fighting.

Rona S., Santa Monica, California

Be careful not to compromise yourself *or* your partner

The longer my partner Kevin and I are together, the more I cannot imagine life without him. I think there are many reasons we'll be together for the rest of our lives, many elements that make our relationship work.

While every relationship involves compromise, both of us have a deep respect for the others' identity and never ask for compromise on things that are core to the other's being. In fact, we're very careful to communicate to one another about the things that are most important to us, and to seek out one another's support.

Lots of times, compromise is easy. For instance, in figuring out who will do what household chores, or choosing an apartment or house to live in. But the key to compromise, for us, and the key to navigating those times when compromise is too painful, is lots of communication until we both get something we want.

Rosalie R., Urbana, Illinois

After reading this chapter, test your relationship I.Q. with the **Improve Your Relationship QUIZ BOOK,** *then use the* **Improve Your Relationship WORK BOOK** *to work on the areas of your relationship that need a little help, using the simple action items checklist in the book. Both books are available only by visiting http://www.ImproveYourRelationship.com.*

#33: The Duties Rule

Think of chores, tasks and other, sometimes unpleasant, duties as hugs and kisses redeemable when you're off duty.

Stay together by dividing up the dirty dishes and dirty diapers

My husband Adam and I both work full-time jobs. For many years we would come home from work about the same time, but I would prepare all the meals, be responsible for cleaning the house, for doing the laundry and for taking care of the kids. He pitched in every now and then as if he were doing me a favor. I found this more insulting than considerate.

As my job became more demanding I became even more stressed with my second full-time job at home. I tried everything to get him to help out, but he never took me seriously.

Finally, I gave him a choice. We could move to a smaller home, scale back our lifestyles and I could quit my job to take care of the house and family full time, or he could pitch in and do half of the work around the house. Another option was that we could spend most of my salary to hire a full-time housekeeper.

He opted to do half the work. We're now a team and many of the things I once dreaded are now, well, fun—because we're doing them as a team.

Adam has always been a team player at work but it never occurred to him to think of household duties as a job! His new attitude has spilled over into other areas of our relationship, as

well, and we are more of a team in every way. Who would have thought that having to do half as many dirty dishes and dirty diapers could improve a relationship.
Lindsay V., Indianapolis, Indiana

Sometimes bribery works best

I tried unsuccessfully for years to get my husband Dave to help out around the house. Finally when all else failed, I tried bribery.

I'm a Creative Director at work, so I decided to be creative. My offer to him was that for everything he did around the house he would earn a coupon redeemable for bedroom time.

Well, it worked in a big way. We turned a source of frustration into a game and we both won.

Who knew that cleaning the toilets could improve our love life? We now use coupons in other areas of our lives as well and they work as good as gold.
Bridgette C., Pensacola, Florida

It's your duty to keep your relationship alive

For us, a good relationship is about so much more than just mowing the lawn, paying the bills or picking up the dry cleaning. It's so much more than just chores and errands and dividing up the daily duties.

My husband Jerome and I have discussed this often and we believe that we both have a duty to make sure our relationship doesn't just drift away or die a slow death.

How often have you heard divorcing couples say "Our marriage just ran its course," or "We fell out of love, we don't know when or where but the love we once had just died." It happens every day because couples don't care enough or because they assume that relationships just magically take care of themselves. Well, they don't.

Like a child or a house or even a lawn, relationships need constant tending to and it's a couple's duty to tend to its relationship in the same way you tend to all of the other things you love or want to preserve for the future.

We believe our first duty is to our relationship. If that falls apart then none of the other things matter. This is the first relationship rule we live by.

Veronica A., Mobile, Alabama

After reading this chapter, test your relationship I.Q. with the **Improve Your Relationship QUIZ BOOK,** *then use the* **Improve Your Relationship WORK BOOK** *to work on the areas of your relationship that need a little help, using the simple action items checklist in the book. Both books are available only by visiting http://www.ImproveYourRelationship.com.*

#34: The Effort / Willingness Rule

Like good customer service, give more than your partner expects and you'll have a happy customer, and partner, for life.

Just what the relationship doctor ordered

I'm a nurse and I guess it's just in my nature to take care of people. I enjoy it, which is fortunate because my husband Ron likes to be taken care of.

My friends feel that I'm being taken advantage of, but I don't feel I am. I didn't consciously choose him because of his neediness, but perhaps subconsciously I did. We complement each other and for us it's been one of the keys to our very happy 15-year relationship.

If I were also needy, we'd have a problem. But as it is, we're a perfect match—he needs me as much as I need him.

Pamela K., Cheyenne, Wyoming

Use your secret weapon for good

I've found that if I make an effort to give more than 50-percent—more than what I feel is my fair share—in all areas of my relationship, it's almost always returned by my partner. I learned this years ago in my first relationship in high school.

Today I'm married to a wonderful woman. I don't know if it's been out of guilt or out of appreciation, but over the years my wife has come around and now makes more of an effort when it comes to our love life.

With three kids and a home-based freelance part-time job, not to mention a house to keep up, she's pretty exhausted at the end of the day. Romance and affection, more often than not, have ended up at the bottom of her "To-Do" list, which is completely understandable.

Instead of getting angry or resentful, I just decided that whenever I felt like I wasn't getting what I wanted or needed from her, I would just give more, instead of blaming her for not giving enough. I guess some would call it reverse psychology, but I call it my secret weapon. It worked.

Nick B., Billings, Montana

Go on strike

When my partner Dan and I were first dating, we had separate apartments. He did his own shopping, his own laundry and even made his own meals.

When we married I assumed we'd share the household chores. Boy, was I in for a surprise. Soon after the honeymoon, in his eyes I morphed into his mother and was apparently only there to serve his every desire. Unfortunately, this was a big turn-off for me.

I tried everything. I tried talking. I tried getting angry and threatening (much like his mom would have done, I'm guessing). Finally, I decided to go on strike. The dishes piled up, the social engagements were missed and the affection stopped. I got his attention.

Today we have an equal partnership. We both make the effort to keep our relationship on the right track. Like a kid, he was pushing to see what he could get away with. He's not the most mature man in the world, but he makes up for it in other important ways. Equal effort is important to me and today I'd say his reluctant willingness to meet me half way has been the biggest key to our happy relationship.

Patty O., Tyler, Texas

Is "his problem" you?

For years I nagged my husband Richard to share his feelings, to open up, to let me know when he was angry. This only made things worse. He became more and more withdrawn and defensive and we ended up fighting even more. He refused to go to therapy, so I went alone.

After years of frustration I learned to let go. I had become fixated on "his problem" and ignored the problem I was creating. He still keeps his feelings to himself and doesn't communicate as much as I'd like, but I now focus on all of the effort he does make in our relationship. He does make an effort to be a good father to our children and in most ways he's a terrific husband, just not in the ways I wanted him to be.

Once I decided it wasn't worth ruining our good relationship to have what I thought would be a *perfect* relationship (I'm a bit of a control-freak), I was able to let it go. I was spending too much effort trying to change him. Now that I focus that effort on myself, I'm happier with myself and I'm happier in our relationship.

Mara T., Ogden, Utah

After reading this chapter, test your relationship I.Q. with the **Improve Your Relationship QUIZ BOOK,** *then use the* **Improve Your Relationship WORK BOOK** *to work on the areas of your relationship that need a little help, using the simple action items checklist in the book. Both books are available only by visiting http://www.ImproveYourRelationship.com.*

#35: The Manners Rule

Thank your partner for something every day
and your partner will thank your parents
for giving him you.

Politeness and courtesy may seem old-fashioned, but they never go out of style

It may seem trite, but I fell in love with my boyfriend, who's now my husband, because he was so charming and polite. He was pretty sexy too, but that was secondary to me. He really stood out from the other men I had dated.

He's still old-fashioned and opens doors for me and makes me feel special. I learned from his example and now I try every day to thank him for all of the things he does for me.

Dana U., Baltimore, Maryland

Manners make you feel special about that special person in your life

It may seem like a small thing but manners are important in a relationship. Sometimes it's the little behaviors that really tell you how someone feels about you. I was brought up to say please and thank you, my wife wasn't. At the beginning of our relationship I felt that she didn't appreciate the things I did for her. It turns out she did, she just didn't know how to express it. Once she knew it was important to me she made an effort and it's made all the difference in the world.

Keiran O., Lowell, Massachusetts

Would you rather have Popeye or Brutus for a mate?

I used to think that communication and sex and love and all of the other "big things" were what made a relationship happy. But I was wrong.

After many happy years with my husband Matt, I've come to see it's the little things, the things we take for granted—like manners—that are critical to a happy marriage. The big things are only possible because of courtesy, consideration, kindness, respect and other good manners.

I never thought I'd find Matt's good manners sexy, but I do. I'm no Oliveoyle, but I'd much rather spend my life with a polite guy like Popeye than an inconsiderate hunk like Brutus. He may have lots of sexy muscles, but his behavior's not sexy at all.

Lannie F., Norfolk, Virginia

A good relationship can be a scream

These days everyone is so rude. Having to deal with rude drivers on the road, rude salesclerks in stores, rude co-workers and rude neighbors, the last thing I want is to come home to a rude husband.

My husband Derrick tends to be rude and abrupt at times, which used to push my hot buttons, making me lash out or act rude in return. When that happened it would only escalate the situation. For the longest time I tried to get Derrick to deal with his frustration in a more productive, less rude manner, but with no luck. I tried inspiring him, pleading with him, bargaining with him, threatening him, but nothing worked.

Taking his frustrations out on me made me want to scream—so one day, that's what I did. But not at him. I knew that wouldn't help, so instead, I screamed into a pillow. I'd heard that this was a good release and it was.

Now when he displays his bad manners I just give *him* a

pillow to scream into. It took a while for him to try it and to get the hang of it but he eventually embraced it. On our last anniversary I even bought him his own special screaming pillow. I bought a second one for myself. Some couples have his and her towels, we've got his and her frustration-management pillows.

Now, on those rare occasions when he treats me rudely, I just throw him his pillow or pick up mine and scream, rather than respond. He gets the message loud and clear.

Shari U., Brooklyn, New York

After reading this chapter, test your relationship I.Q. with the **Improve Your Relationship QUIZ BOOK,** *then use the* **Improve Your Relationship WORK BOOK** *to work on the areas of your relationship that need a little help, using the simple action items checklist in the book. Both books are available only by visiting http://www.ImproveYourRelationship.com.*

#36: The Maturity Rule

Be patient. Like trees, money-market accounts and fine wine, it may take time for you and your relationship to grow and mature.

It's unfortunate that we so often only learn from our own mistakes, but even more unfortunate when we don't

There's nothing like experience. After being in a few relationships, it's easier to know what it is you want and what you don't want in a mate.

I believe my present relationship is strong, satisfying and happy because we both were in very bad relationships prior to us getting together. Those relationships not only taught us what we didn't want from a partner, but also taught us to appreciate each other more. We don't take each other for granted and we show each other, every day, that we're happy to be together (with hugs, kisses, I love yous and especially compliments).

Both of our prior marriages lasted several years and they were extremely difficult to get out of. We got out of our marriages to be with each other, but we were both miserable before we ever met. We met at work nine years ago. We were just friends for a couple of years, but I had the hots for him for months and months before I ever said anything to him about it. After many, many conversations about our miserable lives, I finally got the courage to tell him how I felt. At that point, I decided that somehow I was leaving my husband, who I was also afraid of.

We didn't start having an affair until after I left my husband. My ex was verbally abusive and lazy (he "worked" from home and was a stay-at-home dad, but wouldn't take care of the household). He was controlling (told me what to wear and what to do), jealous, alcoholic and a drug abuser (pot).

His marriage was loveless, sexless and resentful (they basically just occupied the same house).

My new partner and I appreciate each other even more because it was a very long and difficult process to get here. And not one we'll soon forget.

Joy B., Kansas City, Missouri

You can have a mature relationship at any age

When Larry and I got married I was nineteen-years-old and he was twenty-five. We had only known each other for a few months and despite all the negative opinions from family and friends we knew we were doing the right thing.

We've been married now for 24 years and have three children. One is grown and living on her own and two are teenagers still living at home. We have a relationship that most couples can only dream about.

There are many reasons or "secrets" for having a happy relationship, but one of the most important is one that was given to us on our wedding night by a Methodist minister at a small wedding chapel in Las Vegas, Nevada. After we exchanged vows and before he announced us "Man and Wife," he told us that ahead of us there would be many rocky roads and times in which we would feel like walking away and never looking back. He explained that when we hit one of these rocky roads that we should remember the moment we became man and wife and how much love we had in our hearts for one another and that it would be that love that would get us through.

This was advice that we've held onto and used many

times. This advice has smoothed many rocky roads and as a result we have a strong, solid love for each other that has grown steadily throughout the years.
Amy C., Prescott, Arizona

After reading this chapter, test your relationship I.Q. with the **Improve Your Relationship QUIZ BOOK,** *then use the* **Improve Your Relationship WORK BOOK** *to work on the areas of your relationship that need a little help, using the simple action items checklist in the book. Both books are available only by visiting http://www.ImproveYourRelationship.com.*

#37: The Obligations Rule

When you have to choose between outside obligations such as careers, friends and parents, if you want your relationship to last, always put your partner first.

Spend less time at work and you'll have less work to do at home to patch up your relationship

I have a friend who often complains that she isn't in a relationship. She has a high-powered job that takes her out of the country for months at a time each year and when she's in town she works six days a week, 12 hours a day. She doesn't see that her job *is* her relationship. My friend doesn't have time for a man or a family.

A few years after we were married, my husband was promoted and with the promotion came lots of extra hours. I began to feel like a widow. I reminded Robert that spending time together on a budget was preferable to spending all that extra money he was earning, on a divorce settlement. He agreed and changed jobs. We've been happy ever since.

Elena B., Athens, Georgia

We discovered eight ways to say "I Love You"

Well here I am writing about something that I thought I'd never have, a successful relationship. Especially following two unsuccessful marriages (one to a gambler, and the other to a man who thought he needed more than one woman at a time). Finally, for me, the third time was the charm.

After nine years alone, I met the man who still shares my life. When I met Frank we were both divorced. He had three kids from his marriage and I had five from mine. And believe me, we weren't *The Brady Bunch.*

It was very difficult at times for us and the kids. Mixing two families isn't easy. We had to have patience and understanding and nerves of steel. After a few rough times we finally figured out how to make things work. We agreed that our first obligation was accept each other's previous obligations and to help each other live up to our obligations. He accepts my sons for who they are and thinks of them as his own. We had a more difficult time getting his daughters to accept me, but now they're like my own.

This was the first and highest hurdle in our relationship. It was challenging, but well worth it. Patience, understanding and working as a team worked then and it still works for us today, now that we're retired.

Pat G., Quartzsite, Arizona

Do you follow the crowd or lead?

For years I dragged my husband, against his will, to family holiday gatherings, to my company get-togethers, to weddings and funerals and to other obligations of mine that were miserable wastes of time for him. And he returned the favor.

Finally, one day we asked each other why we were doing this. Was it because that's what we thought we were supposed to do as a couple? Was it because it's what everyone else does? We realized we were just blindly following the crowd and decided to stop.

There are occasions, special times, that for personal reasons we want the other to attend one of those obligatory functions, but for the most part attending them alone is just fine and sometimes even preferable. For instance, you don't have to spend time worrying about whether or not the other is having a good time. But best of all, we now no longer have to feel guilty about forcing the other to do something he or she doesn't want to do.

I believe we've had a happy relationship because we don't just blindly follow the crowd. We question convention and expectations and decide for ourselves what's right for us. It's worked well for 14 years, so we must be doing something right.

Diana J., Philadelphia, Pennsylvania

After reading this chapter, test your relationship I.Q. with the **Improve Your Relationship QUIZ BOOK**, *then use the* **Improve Your Relationship WORK BOOK** *to work on the areas of your relationship that need a little help, using the simple action items checklist in the book. Both books are available only by visiting http://www.ImproveYourRelationship.com.*

#38: The Temptations Rule

If your partner's getting what he or she wants
at home there's no reason to look for it outside.
Don't have to hold on too tight to your mate.
Just be so irresistable that you'll be your
mates biggest temptation.

Don't let yourself go, if you don't want your partner to go

My wife is very attractive, has a great body and loves to
flirt. She says it's innocent fun but for the first few years of our
marriage it drove me crazy. I was jealous and always afraid she
would find someone better. She stopped flirting—at least when
I was around—but I couldn't get her to wear a Burkha!

I felt helpless. I wanted to do something but I didn't know
what. Then one day, out of the blue, it came to me. I decided to
stop worrying about all the other guys in the world and to
concentrate on me.

She married me because I had all the qualities she wanted
in a man. So I reasoned, if she's getting what she wants at
home there's no reason for her to look for it outside.

Most of the guys I know, once they're married, let themselves go. I guess they think they don't have to try anymore to
keep their wives attracted or interested. For us, that's been the
key. If I'm giving her my best and it isn't enough, well, I can't
worry about that.

Anton Y., Natchez, Louisiana

Don't make it too easy for them to leave

My advice is NEVER allow any woman to be so comfortable in your home that she feels she lives there and is entitled to anything she wants—mainly, your husband!

My husband left me and my two teenage children, after many years of marriage, for our neighbor and "good friend," who lived across the street. My husband is still married to her, and they have children together, but he now secretly visits me. I've become the other woman.

RoseMarie L. B., Saddlebrook, New Jersey

Just because it's natural doesn't means its inevitable

After 25 years of marriage, we are fully aware of and accept the fact that as humans we will be physically attracted to other people. Because we're aware of this we both know the importance of not allowing ourselves to be in a position that may promote extra-marital affairs. If we find ourselves in a possibly compromising position we get out immediately. It's very important to never put yourself in a position that may lead to temptation.

We're both very sexual people and have an extremely active sex life that has always remained monogamous. The "secret" is we know the difference between romantic sex, emotional sex and sex. We still practice all three.

Amy C., Prescott, Arizona

Peer-pressure proof your relationship

Over and over, studies show that when children have two loving parents who spend lots of time with them, encourage them, support them and communicate openly with them they are much less likely to be tempted by peer pressure.

Children who are close to their parents and feel love and respected by their parents are not tempted to take drugs, to smoke, to drink or to act out in school. These kids fit in at home and don't need to act out to fit in with their peers.

The same is true in a marriage or relationship. If you're part of a safe, loving and an open environment at home, you won't be tempted by money or power or sex or drugs or other adult peer pressures. It's only when you aren't getting what you want that you're vulnerable to these everyday temptations.

To avoid them, find out what your partner wants and isn't getting and give it to him. Then tell him what you want. Chances are high you'll get it, if you're willing to give first. Most of us just don't ask, or if we do, it's in the wrong way.

Curtis K., Miami, Florida

After reading this chapter, test your relationship I.Q. with the **Improve Your Relationship QUIZ BOOK,** *then use the* **Improve Your Relationship WORK BOOK** *to work on the areas of your relationship that need a little help, using the simple action items checklist in the book. Both books are available only by visiting http://www.ImproveYourRelationship.com.*

Section 7
The Sex Challenge

Follow these four simple rules if you want
to create Relationship Magic

#39: The Affection / Intimacy Rule

Unlike football, in the game of love you score extra points for holding. When it comes to affection, intimacy and love, it's always more important to show it than to say it.

Add a few kisses to your "To Do" list

We have a rule at our house that no one come or goes without a kiss. On the weekends when there are lots of errands that find us coming and going, there are lots of kisses. It makes having to do those chores not so bad.

One of the side benefits is that if something is bothering you, you try to clear it up right away. After all, it's not fun to kiss someone you're angry with. So the kissing rule is good motivation to solve issues early, before they grow.

Stephen J., Pasadena, California

Learning the body language of love

Sex is great, but we don't always have the time or the place or even the energy. Holding hands, however, can be done anywhere and at anytime.

My husband Christopher and I hold hands in the park, in the car, at the movies, at PTA meetings and just about everywhere. We started holding hands when we were first dating and never stopped.

I love telling the world that "I'm with him." And whenever one of us doesn't want to hold hands we know it means the other is upset or needs to talk. We don't even have to say a

word to know something is wrong. It's our personal sign language. It's one of those small things that means a lot.
Brittany D., Portland, Maine

Love is an act, not a feeling

It's the acts of love that we demonstrate, that bond us together. Hugs and kisses go a long way. A compliment will be heard. Some people don't recite from the "Book Of Sweet Nothings" but love deeply.

Sometimes the people who say that they love you with ease are often those who cannot love deeply. An example is the battering husband who says he loves his wife after he hits her. The wife who has an affair but professes to love her husband. These people don't act in a loving manner but the words pour like honey from their mouths.

The clinical definition of love is when the other person's well being is more important or equal to your own. Would the man who says he loves you donate his kidney to save you? Would the woman who loves you forgive you if you made a mistake? I found it's the loving *acts* that make us feel important in our lover's eyes.
Sally S., Toronto, Ontario, Canada

Cuddle up to your canary

Affection is like a canary in a coal mine. When it dies the relationship usually follows.

My wife Dorie and I take a couple of hours every night to hug and hold hands and cuddle on the couch while we watch television or a movie. We unplug the phone and don't answer the door. It's our time together and it's our favorite time of each day. With our stressful lives it's the perfect stress relief and something to look forward to each day.
Brad H., Davenport, Iowa

Learning to be affectionate is kids play

Both my husband Bobby and I grew up in families that were pretty non-affectionate. This is one of the bonds we share. I can say without a doubt that our kids aren't being raised without affection and that really makes us happy. It's a shared goal.

Marcia S., Bakersfield, California

Make your own house calls

For years we found it was rare when both of us were in the mood for sex at the same time. It always seemed like such a chore to plan and initiate. All the fun was gone. Then we discovered massage. We both have stressful jobs, like most everyone these days, and found that massage was a great way to relax and relieve the tension.

We also discovered, by accident, that it often puts us both in the mood. So now, two or three times a week we take time to massage each other. Full body massages, lying on a bed often naturally leads to more. But even when it doesn't, it still keeps us close and intimate—and out of the chiropractor's and therapist's office. That's what I call a bargain.

Donnie D., Tuscaloosa, Alabama

After reading this chapter, test your relationship I.Q. with the **Improve Your Relationship QUIZ BOOK,** *then use the* **Improve Your Relationship WORK BOOK** *to work on the areas of your relationship that need a little help, using the simple action items checklist in the book. Both books are available only by visiting http://www.ImproveYourRelationship.com.*

#40: The Mystery Rule

Even the best mystery book ever written gets boring once you've read it a few times. To create a little mystery in the bedroom, change the plot, add a few kinks to the characters and keep your partner guessing.

Become the mystery man or woman

If it's true that passion fades after you become familiar with one another then why not confuse or surprise your partner and rekindle his or her interest?

If you've never taken a shower together, surprise him some morning. If you've worn the same hair-style or had the same hair color for years, change it. (Blondes do have more fun, by the way.)

If you have a set routine he knows he can count on, alter it. But be prepared. He may ask if you're having an affair. When you confess that you are and that it's with *him* you'll both remember what it's like to be infatuated all over again.

Over the years my husband and I have made surprising each other a game. It's fun, it's easy and we both get to win.

Chandra P., St. Petersburg, Florida

If you ever want to do it again make your mate ask whodunit

It's a mystery to me why so many of our coupled friends have lost all the mystery and excitement in their love lives. There are so many ways to create a little mystery in the love life department.

165

Every month my wife and I have a mystery date. We take turns planning it. We go away for the weekend, but only one of us knows where we're going, where we'll eat, where we'll stay. Sometimes it's local, sometimes it's a plane trip or a cruise.

Spending the weekend in a mysterious destination, sleeping in strange beds and not knowing what will come next is a ritual that has kept our relationship not only full of mystery but full of anticipation, looking forward to the next mysterious outing.

Christian T., Las Vegas, Nevada

After reading this chapter, test your relationship I.Q. with the **Improve Your Relationship QUIZ BOOK,** *then use the* **Improve Your Relationship WORK BOOK** *to work on the areas of your relationship that need a little help, using the simple action items checklist in the book. Both books are available only by visiting http://www.ImproveYourRelationship.com.*

#41: The Passion Rule

Despite what you may have heard, it doesn't have to end after the honeymoon. If you can stay passionate about your hobbies, Monday Night Football and politics, you can remain passionate about your partner.

Change your routine before it becomes routine

Sometimes keeping the passion alive is as simple as changing your routine.

Once a week my wife Yolanda and I meet somewhere different to make love. We take turns choosing the location. Hotels, the back seat of our minivan, on a sailboat, in the woods, in a pool, in a tent—we've tried it all. It's surprising what a turn-on it is to do it in a sleeping bag under the stars.

Some guys get passionate about sports; I get passionate about scoring with my favorite team mate.

Damian Q., Pocatello, Idaho

Make an appointment with passion

To keep the passion alive, my husband and I make, what we like to call, "Passion Appointments."

Ari and I both have busy schedules and stressful jobs, so we have to make time rather than waiting for the right time. Making love in the middle of the day on a Wednesday, or at midnight on Monday can be a thrill. As long as every week is different, it always seems exciting.

Sometimes we make an early breakfast-in-bed appointment. Still, at other times we'll schedule an afternoon quickie in his office.

Instead of using our hectic, demanding jobs as an excuse to avoid sex, we use them as an excuse to keep the passion alive.

Anna N., Cedar Rapids, Iowa

You don't need Viagra to be intimate 24 hours a day

After 20 years of marriage my husband Evan and I are still very much in love. We kiss and hug and cuddle daily but very rarely go "all the way" anymore.

My girlfriends think something must be wrong and that we can't be happy or in love if we don't have sex. They think that we must be missing something. But we're not.

I admit we both just have low sex drives, but sex really isn't the point. My friends put sex high on their list, but other than sex, their relationships are loveless.

I rarely if ever see my couple friends kiss or hug or hold hands or cuddle. They don't demonstrate much intimacy in their lives so sex becomes the only way for them to connect and it validates their relationships. They use sex to prove to themselves that they're loved.

I think there's too much emphasis on "doing it" and not enough on feeling it and living it. Just turn on a TV set or go to a movie to see what I mean. It doesn't seem to matter how you treat your partner anymore, as long as you get laid.

Good sex lasts a matter of minutes, while intimacy can last all day, every day. If I have to choose, I'll take the intimacy.

Drew K., Spokane, Washington

After reading this chapter, test your relationship I.Q. with the **Improve Your Relationship QUIZ BOOK,** *then use the* **Improve Your Relationship WORK BOOK** *to work on the areas of your relationship that need a little help, using the simple action items checklist in the book. Both books are available only by visiting http://www.ImproveYourRelationship.com.*

#42: The Romance Rule

Do something romantic every day
and you'll improve your relationship
in 365 ways each year.

Lubricate your romance reflex before it begins to squeak

Romance is like lubricant on a rusty door hinge. The door may work just fine but a little grease can get rid of the irritating squeak and make it open and close a lot more smoothly.

Whether it's a romantic weekend getaway or a romantic walk along the beach at sunset every now and then, it's kept our relationship well-oiled. Our marriage would probably still be happy without the romance, but that's exactly why the romance is so important. We do it because we want to, not because we need to or have to. This makes it all the more special and romantic.

Cory L., La Jolla, California

Rich rewards are to be found in reckless acts of romance

For me, it's the random acts of romance that have made our relationship so special over the years. I'm not talking about romance for the purpose of having sex, but the small, unexpected gestures.

Holding hands in the grocery store, catching my husband watching me from across the room at a crowded party, opening the book I've left on my nightstand to find a pressed rose. We could easily have let the passion die years ago, but the romance has kept it alive. It doesn't have to cost anything and it only takes a few minutes, but to your relationship it's worth all the hours in your day and all the money in your bank account.

Paulette P., Little Rock, Arkansas

Buddies are fine, but snuggle buddies are better

After five years together, it's still important to us that our relationship includes a commitment to intimacy. Things can get crazy, we're tired or busy—but it's important for us to remember that our relationship is not only emotional and logistical (living together, sharing a car), it's romantic, too.

Whether that means having sex or just making sure to snuggle in at bedtime, intimacy is the difference between being best friends and being life partners. Both are important—and isn't it lucky to have both in the same person?

Rosalie R., Urbana, Illinois

It's easy to be a 24/7 romantic

When we first met, I thought romance was about giving her flowers, candy and maybe a dinner by candlelight. That was the extent of my romantic experience.

Angeline taught me that romance is about not taking each other for granted. It's about giving your partner your time and your attention. It's about making an effort to make your partner feel special—and you don't even need flowers, candy or candlelit dinners.

Anything can be romantic if you treat it as such. Scaling fish by moonlight, champagne from two styrofoam cups in a hospital room, even sitting in the back row of traffic school holding hands. It's not the place or the activity, it's your intention. Every day and every night can be romantic, why wait for special events?

That's what Angeline and I have done for all of these years

and it's made us very happy.

We've been married for nearly 20 years and we're just as romantic today as we were when we first started dating. But I have to admit, I learned everything I know about romance from her.

Alex Z., Albany, New York

After reading this chapter, test your relationship I.Q. with the **Improve Your Relationship QUIZ BOOK,** *then use the* **Improve Your Relationship WORK BOOK** *to work on the areas of your relationship that need a little help, using the simple action items checklist in the book. Both books are available only by visiting http://www.ImproveYourRelationship.com.*

Section 8
The Love Challenge

Follow these nine simple rules if you want
to discover Relationship Bliss

#43: The Acceptance Rule

You may wish your partner was a king, but
if you can accept that he's just a knight,
you'll enjoy it more when you jump him.
Accept the things you can't change.

Save your fantasies for the bedroom

If you marry a Clark Kent, don't expect him to turn into
Superman. Your life is not a comic book, a TV show or a
movie. That's the mistake I made and it was unfair to my Clark
Kent. It kept us from having a good relationship for years.

The fact is, Clark Kent is a kind and wonderful person with
lots of terrific qualities and Superman probably has more than
a few annoying habits. No one's perfect, we all have our
strengths and weaknesses. It took me many years to be honest
with myself about what I really wanted in a relationship. And
it took years for me to let a real man love me. Luckily, my Clark
had the patience of a man of steel and he put up with me.

It's so much easier to fall in love and be with a Super Hero
and a Fantasy Man, than to love and be satisfied with a mere
mortal.

The irony is that once I accepted my partner for who he
was he became my real life Superman in all the ways that
really matter.

Mary "Lois" L., Fort Wayne, Indiana

On a scale of 1-to-10, what are you willing to accept?

If you've tried telling your partner what you want, asking

for what you want, bargaining and negotiating for what you want, and you still can't get him to budge, then you have two choices. You can leave, or you can accept the situation as it is. But first, you have to ask yourself, on a scale of 1-to-10, how important is this to me?

Not getting what you want in a relationship doesn't make for a happy relationship. Not being able to leave or let go, refusing to accept reality, and fighting it only creates misery. Now you may get some joy out of making your partner miserable for not giving you what you want, but guess what, you're miserable too. So now, not only do you not get what you want, but you've made matters even worse, not your partner.

My partner Tad and I have been together 11 years and we use the 1-to-10 score whenever we negotiate or ask for what we want from one another. If I say this is an eight for me, Tad knows it's to his advantage to give in this time, especially if it's only a six for him. If it's a 10 for him, then it's my cue to give in. If it's a 10 for both of us, we're in trouble or we have to get creative and come up with a solution, which we always seem to manage, when we want to.

To get what you want, you have to know how important it is to your partner, before you start negotiating. This has been our secret and it works nine times out of 10.

Jonathan S., San Jose, California

Is your mate's communication style half full or half empty?

After 22 years of marriage, I try to appreciate what I have instead of complaining about what I don't have in my relationship. And, of course, I try to accept the things I can't change. For instance, most straight men just aren't willing, or able, to express their feelings. They just aren't comfortable talking about "feelings." But they always show you how they feel. Since I put more emphasis on action rather than words, anyway, that works just fine for both of us.

Barbara M., Apple Valley, California

Are you cheating on your partner with his fantasy double?

I had a 19-year marriage. During that time I found that to continue to love him over the years I had to come to love him as he was, not as I would have liked him to be. I forgave him for the things that irritated me the most, and allowed him to change and grow. Because of this, I was happy and had a very happy partner. Nagging them to change never works.

Helen Y., the Internet

Are you a victim of the toothpaste on the bathroom mirror syndrome?

Like the current White House resident has said about global warming, LEARN TO LIVE WITH IT. That's my motto for a happy relationship. I call it the "toothpaste on the bathroom mirror syndrome."

My partner has habits that drive me up the wall. (On the other hand, I can't imagine a single thing that I do that would irritate anyone in the slightest.) I nagged him about certain things in the first year or so but the behavior continued. So, I just shut up and learned to live with it, especially the petty toothpaste on the mirror behavior. I save my nagging for the major stuff and I saved our relationship.

Bill D., Seattle, Washington

For a new perspective, stand back a little further and look at the big picture

A relationship biggie for me is acceptance. In the past, for me, it's been a real struggle. Now, however, before I get mad at something my husband says or does, I ask myself, "Will this really matter 20 years from now?" The answer is almost always NO. Just accepting that some things will probably never change or that I won't eventually get what I want, in some areas, has been helpful and made our lives happier.

Marcia S., Bakersfield, California

After reading this chapter, test your relationship I.Q. with the **Improve Your Relationship QUIZ BOOK,** *then use the* **Improve Your Relationship WORK BOOK** *to work on the areas of your relationship that need a little help, using the simple action items checklist in the book. Both books are available only by visiting http://www.ImproveYourRelationship.com.*

#44: The Appreciation Rule

If you want your relationship to appreciate in value, show your appreciation. Start with a compliment a day. A little interest adds up to a lot over time.

Put on the brakes or you'll miss the appreciation rest stop

I think it's harder for young people to connect today. Everything in our society is geared toward instant gratification. We no longer take the time to get to know one another or to work through problems. How can you appreciate a beautiful flower by the side of the road if you're driving by at 70 miles per hour?

My husband Harry and I have what we call "appreciation moments." Every day I try to take a moment to let Harry know how much I appreciate him, or something he's done, or just that he's in my life. And he does the same for me. We all want to be appreciated but it's so easy to forget to show our appreciation to someone else.

Harry and I have been happily married for just over 50 years and few days have gone by without one of us expressing our appreciation for the other. That's the rule we live by.

Lena B., Salt Lake City, Utah

If you don't want it to end, start with "thank you"

Sometimes we forget that it's very hard, if not impossible, to find someone that we can be extremely happy with. So if you're lucky enough to find that special person who you're very happy and compatible with, you need to treat them like they're your knight in shining armor, so to speak, and let them know how much they're loved everyday. That's what we do and it's worked for us.

Nobody's perfect and yes, if I could, I'd change a few things about my knight, but they're such minor things, that in the big picture, they really aren't that important. And what good would come of me denting his armor?

Joy B., Kansas City, Missouri

Try this miracle cure for your ailing relationship

Most couples I know dislike dealing with problems, differences of opinion and the everyday difficulties that come up in any relationship. Most of these couples are also not what I would call happy.

Over the years I've found that to appreciate anything in life it has to be something you've earned, something you've worked hard for. Of course we can all appreciate a beautiful sunset and the many wonders and miracles of life without doing anything, but the things we cherish most are the things we had to struggle to obtain or achieve.

I'm sure it sounds odd, but I actually look forward to problems because I now know that they're really opportunities for Susan and me to appreciate each other and our relationship.

The unhappy couples we know avoid problems like the plague. We couldn't be happier and perhaps it's because we welcome problems like a miracle cure or or antidote.

Scott D., Providence, Rhode Island

After reading this chapter, test your relationship I.Q. with the **Improve Your Relationship QUIZ BOOK,** *then use the* **Improve Your Relationship WORK BOOK** *to work on the areas of your relationship that need a little help, using the simple action items checklist in the book. Both books are available only by visiting http://www.ImproveYourRelationship.com.*

#45: The Consideration Rule

It's 8:00 pm, do you know where your partner is?
Don't take him or her for granted.

Show me, don't tell me

One night, after a year or so of marriage, my husband was feeling romantic, or maybe just horny. I remember he looked into my eyes and said "I love you." I looked back and asked him why he hadn't called to let me know he would be two hours late, or why he had eaten the last brownie (the ones I baked and hadn't yet tasted).

Well, I ruined the mood, but I made my point—and he got it. My philosophy is, show me, don't tell me. Words are cheap. It's made all the difference in our relationship and in him reevaluating his philosophy.

Mary Ann M., Muncie, Indiana

Your cell phone—don't leave home without it

I was a stay-at-home-mom for many years and loved it. My husband Harry was busy in his business and that was okay with me. His business was in sales and often meant time away from home. I covered the bases as a baseball mother and then did all the stuff at school that mom's do.

Harry had five salesmen working for him and one night they went to a meeting and didn't return until much later than usual. Each of their wives called late that night wondering what had happened to their husbands. Cell phones weren't yet invented.

All of the wives lost a night of sleep and spent the night worrying about their husbands. We later learned that the men had continued their meeting in the parking lot, at their car doors and simply lost track of time. It was as simple as that.

After that incident I decided I wouldn't worry or lose sleep unless I found a reason to worry. I never found a reason for distrust and I never lost a night of sleep again. Of course I missed him when he was away on business, but after that night, even though he knew I trusted him, he always called to let me know where and how he was.

Lillian S., San Jacinto, California

Being considerate is the best way to say "I love you"

I buy a new car every 15 to 20 years. For me cars are a necessity. I get no thrill handing over my money to buy something that depreciates before you drive off the lot.

My partner Freddie on the other hand loves to blow money. Especially on cars. Until we met, he bought a new car every two years. Now he only buys a new car every four years or so. I guess I've had a small influence on him.

Last year I told him that the next time he was ready to buy a new car to let me know and I would buy his. Since he always trades them in to the dealer for Blue Book price I told him I'd give him the same amount in cash.

A few months later, he went out for errands on a Saturday morning and didn't return until that evening. This wasn't like him and I was worried. He had a cellphone but didn't call. That night he pulled into the driveway with a beautiful new car.

I was hurt on so many levels that I couldn't even speak. It was clear that he had been planning this purchase, in secret, for months and never mentioned it. He wanted to have fun blowing his money and didn't want me to ruin his fun.

Freddie says "I love you" almost every day but his actions quite often say just the opposite. On this day his actions said "screw you, it's my money and my car and I'll do what I want to."

As far as I was concerned he had told me loud and clear that I wasn't important and that we really didn't have the relationship I thought we had. When I calmly asked him if our relationship was over, it hit him what he had done. He realized he was going to have plenty of room in our two car garage to park his new car. When he realized how hurt I was and that I was halfway out the door, he understood what he had done to our relationship and apologized. It took a while but I forgave him.

Today our relationship is stronger because he realizes that being considerate is the best way to say "I love you."

Robin F., Fresno, California

You don't have to say a word to say "I love you."

I used to be married to a woman who'd say "I love you" as easily as she said "Hello" or "Goodbye." The trouble was, her behaviors were anything but loving. Her words were hollow.

We divorced after she ran up a $20,000 credit card bill. It was an expensive lesson, but I learned what to look for.

My new wife demonstrates her love daily, without a word. We reserve "I love you" for special occasions.

Liam O., Rapid City, South Dakota

After reading this chapter, test your relationship I.Q. with the **Improve Your Relationship QUIZ BOOK**, *then use the* **Improve Your Relationship WORK BOOK** *to work on the areas of your relationship that need a little help, using the simple action items checklist in the book. Both books are available only by visiting http://www.ImproveYourRelationship.com.*

#46: The Forgiveness Rule

In the game of love, everyone fumbles and drops
the ball at one time or another. Unless your partner's
flaws are illegal, immoral, unethical or dangerous,
everyone deserves a second chance.

**If you want to be together in the future, forgive your
partner's mistakes of the past**

My partner and I had a thirty-eight year relationship until
he died of lung cancer four years ago. I'm still devastated.

Forgiveness was our secret. Ultimately, as we grew older, it
was genuine affection (as opposed to passionate love) with lots
of touching and reminiscing that made us happy.

But most of all we found it helped to forget anything bad
that we may have done to each other over the years.

Jim D. M., New York, New York

**Before you can worship your relationship, you need to
forgive yourself**

Forgiving yourself is even more important than forgiving
your partner. In the past, when my husband Aidan did something to hurt me, whether intentional or unintentional, instead
of expressing my hurt, anger or disappointment, or even
letting it go, I would hold on to it and hold a grudge.

It took me years of therapy to realize that holding a grudge
was my way of keeping the anger focused on him instead of
on me, where it belonged. I was really angry at myself for not
speaking up, for allowing myself to be treated in a way that I

didn't want to be treated and for not doing anything to stop it. Once I learned to forgive myself I was able to stop being passive/aggressive towards Aidan.

Holding a grudge is like paying for a bad dinner with a credit card and then each month making only the minimum payments on the credit card. You just keep paying over and over for the same meal that the made you sick in the first place. And to add insult to injury, you're also paying exorbitant interest rates each month.

The first step to forgiving your partner is to forgive yourself.

Claudia C., Buffalo, New York

Don't ruin your relationship over a toilet seat

Don't let the little things bother you. We live in a world of uncertainty. Who knows how long any of us will be together? So why let little things come between us? Solve the little problems in simple ways. There are enough big things to concern us all.

So if he leaves his socks on the floor, pick them up and put them in the hamper. If he leaves the seat up in the bathroom, close it. I've learned over the years, not to whittle away at our love with the little annoying things of everyday life.

Bea S., Manchester, Connecticut

You may win the grudge match, but all you win is the boobie prize

Forgiveness is important in any relationship. It isn't enough to say, "I forgive you." In fact, sometimes those words can be self-serving and hurtful.

Forgiveness means not holding a grudge, giving up feeling hurt or feeling offended. This may take some work, but from my experience, it's worth it if the relationship is really import-

ant to you.
Peggy S., Park City, Utah

Forgiving is letting them off the hook. Forgetting is letting yourself off the hook

After being married for 10 years my husband Blake cheated on me with my best friend.

Some people say they'll forgive but they'll never forget. I think they've got it backwards. I'll never forgive, but I can forget, now that it's been a couple of years, and move on.

I'll never forgive him for what he did—there's absolutely no excuse for what he did. That doesn't mean, however, that we can't have a happy relationship.

Blake owned up to what he did and apologized. I dealt with my hurt and anger and have let it go. I don't punish him or hold a grudge. I don't let this contaminate the other areas of our relationship. I stay with him because I love him, because we have children, because we have a history and because we enjoy being together. But he also knows that if he ever does it again I'll leave without hesitation.

Forgiving is letting them off the hook. Forgetting is letting yourself off the hook. I'm not going to punish myself for my partner's unforgivable act.

This is an extreme example, but there are many minor things in a marriage that you need to let go of. If you can't let go you can't have a happy relationship. This is my secret.
Melanie B., Portland, Oregon

After reading this chapter, test your relationship I.Q. with the **Improve Your Relationship QUIZ BOOK,** *then use the* **Improve Your Relationship WORK BOOK** *to work on the areas of your relationship that need a little help, using the simple action items checklist in the book. Both books are available only by visiting http://www.ImproveYourRelationship.com.*

#47: The Friendship Rule

Falling in love with someone is like riding a bike, just about anyone can do it. Getting to know someone and becoming friends first is more like the Tour de France. It takes more time but if you're willing, you're much more likely to eventually cross the finish line.

Make sure you like the person you fall in love with

It's been almost a year now since I met Mr. Right and we moved in together. We've had some bumps in the road and there are times when life's trials have made us unhappy. But we've been able to talk about everything, and we've supported each other and been there for each other even when it's seemed the whole rest of the world was against us.

During these hardest times it's been the most obvious to me that I've found my best friend, that nothing can tear us apart. I've become an even stronger person because I know he's always got my back. I'm emotionally secure, because I know nothing will make him stop loving me. I love myself more, because his respect for me has shown me what a good person I am. And life is so much more fun, because he still makes me laugh everyday, out loud and from my gut.

Stefanie R., Carrboro, North Carolina

Sometimes it's more important to like each other than to love each other—love's the easy part

I'm on my third marriage and this is the best relationship I've ever been in. We like each other. We trust each other. We like to be around each other. We don't try to "entertain" or "work" at our relationship. Before we became intimate (not sexually) with each other, we both realized that we could live in peace with the other.

Due to my past marriages and children there have been events that tested our commitment to each other, and we've passed, because of our friendship.

Mike E., Tucson, Arizona

Try a little friendly persuasion

I know many couples who seem to love each other but who don't really seem to like each other very much. Their relationships are passionate and volatile and full of trauma but lack caring and reliability and honesty. And honesty is so important in any good relationship.

Who's better than a friend to tell you the truth, to call you on the carpet when you need it? If you can't count on your friends to be honest with you, who can you count on? The same holds true for your spouse.

Like the friends I still have from high school, my husband Giovanni and I still like each other, still find each other interesting and still enjoy just being together after all of these years.

Being friends *and* lovers is a relationship bonus and it's kept us happy for 29 years. If you aren't friends with your partner, but want to be, then do what a friend does, be a good friend.

Sophie P., Winnipeg, Manitoba, Canada

After reading this chapter, test your relationship I.Q. with the **Improve Your Relationship QUIZ BOOK,** *then use the* **Improve Your Relationship WORK BOOK** *to work on the areas of your relationship that need a little help, using the simple action items checklist in the book. Both books are available only by visiting http://www.ImproveYourRelationship.com.*

#48: The Giving Rule

Give what you want to get—and be the first one to do it. In addition, give what your partner wants, not just what you want to give.

Give your partner the benefit of the doubt and act "as if"

My partner Sterling and I have been together for 19 years. One of the most powerful things I've learned during this time is to say "I love you" or to express my love, even when I'm not in the mood or when I find him annoying. It makes Sterling feel better, I feel better about myself, and it stops me from being petty. Maybe not at the moment, but in hindsight, I'm always glad I acted "as if."

Flavio S., Tucson, Arizona

The more you give, the more you get back

A successful relationship is two-way. A selfish, infantile person will never give back to you, and giving is the key. If you try to have a long-term relationship with such a person, you'll find yourself doing all the giving, and that puts a strain on your ability to love.

Looks and charm aren't everything. After a while, an ugly person you love looks beautiful to you. Likewise, a person with great physical beauty can appear ugly to you if all of your experiences with him or her are negative.

Peggy S., Park City, Utah

Give them gifts they won't want to return

Some people only give gifts that they enjoy buying or would enjoy getting. They don't stop to ask "What would my partner want?"

I have to admit I used to be like this. Granted, my husband is a difficult person to buy for, but I was a selfish gift giver. I love shopping for clothes and personal items. He prefers practical gifts. For a long time I gave him things I knew he wouldn't want because they made *me* feel good to buy. And I felt he *should* want them. After all, they were gifts from the heart. Instead of being a celebration, gift giving would always turn into disappointment, for both of us.

It took me a long time to understand that the most wonderful, thoughtful gift in the world isn't if you know it's something your partner doesn't want. In fact, it's not a gift at all. The best gift is being considerate of what your partner needs and desires. Once I learned this our relationship improved dramatically, because it applies to so many other areas of a marriage, as well.

Keri M., Hilo, Hawaii

Every day's a reason to celebrate couples day

Boy, were we on a tight budget when we first met in college. We couldn't afford expensive gifts, so instead, we skipped traditional birthday and holiday gifts and started giving each other simple gifts from the heart every day.

We gave each other things that didn't cost anything, such as a flower picked from the garden, a poem, a meaningful cartoon clipped from a newspaper, or a special meal, for example. These gifts usually only took a few minutes to find or to make but they stayed with us all day long. And it was fun to come up with new gifts every day.

Even though we can now both afford expensive gifts,

we've stuck with our tradition of giving a daily inexpensive or free gift that means more to us than any diamond ring or expensive concert tickets ever could.

Emily W., Raleigh, North Carolina

After reading this chapter, test your relationship I.Q. with the **Improve Your Relationship QUIZ BOOK,** *then use the* **Improve Your Relationship WORK BOOK** *to work on the areas of your relationship that need a little help, using the simple action items checklist in the book. Both books are available only by visiting http://www.ImproveYourRelationship.com.*

#49: The Kindness Rule

Be as kind to your partner as you are to puppies and children and his or her love for you will grow as fast as puppies and children do. And remember, nice guys may finish last in business, but not in love. Never do anything that would hurt your partner.

Youthful acts of kindness

I'm in my 40's, I'm still attractive, and because of my profession have lots of opportunities to meet beautiful young women. I've also had many opportunities to sleep with them. But I never have.

Not that I haven't been tempted. Instead, I share each flirtation or come-on with my wife. I'm flattered by the attention and that I'm still desirable to someone other than my wife, and she's flattered that I continue to find her more desirable, after nine years of marriage, than a one-night stand.

It's ironic that instead of being a threat to our marriage, the situation is a turn-on for me and my wife. The bottom line is I would never do anything that would harm my wife or our relationship and I know she wouldn't either.

Brett P., San Diego, California

It's okay to be stupid or foolish, but not hurtful

My partner, John, and I have been together for just over 30 years now. When we met I thought I'd met the perfect Prince Charming. Before long I discovered that while he was charming, he wasn't always a prince. And neither was I. But I wanted to have a relationship with a human being and had to let him be human. I didn't get it right all the time, and neither did he. But I gave him room.

There are times when we might use words, always regretted later, during a heated argument, but that doesn't happen very often. When either of us really messes up, it has never been with the intention of hurting, shortchanging, or deceiving the other. We have known couples who have done things like destroy valued photos, sell heirloom jewelry, burn the other's clothing, all kinds of spiteful stuff, with the sole intention of hurting their mate. Their relationships didn't last.

I've been known to do foolish things like go out drinking with friends and overspend on the budget. Sometimes that means next week's entertainment, or the new shoes we had hoped to purchase, is postponed or canceled. Does this have consequences on John? Of course it does. But although it makes him angry and me guilty, and even if we have a snit about it, we both know that it was done because of my weakness, not because I wanted to hurt him.

Bill D., Seattle Washington

Bake yourself a kindness cake and celebrate

Kindness gets little respect these days, but I believe it's the most underrated behavior in a relationship and the key to a happy one. The saying "Nice guys finish last" may be true about the dog-eat-dog, cut-throat world of business, but not about relationships. In fact, a nice guy always finishes first when his partner is a nice gal (or guy, depending on your orientation). If you're a kind lover, your lover will always come back for more.

Kindness from a partner allows us to be ourselves and inspires us to be our best selves because we know that we won't be put down or embarrassed or criticized by our partner.

Kindness is like water or flour in a recipe. It's an ingredient we take for granted and rarely even consider. It doesn't get noticed like hot spices or exotic flavors, but it holds the entire recipe together.

For years I dated hot, spicy and exotic men who were exciting, powerful, and adventurous, but none of them were marriage material. When I was ready to settle down I chose a sweet, kind man with a great sense of humor.

He may not be powerful or exciting or spicy in the traditional sense but he's the icing on my cake.

If you're already in a relationship with one of those exciting, powerful and adventurous types who's less than kind, it's not hopeless. Most decent people become better when they interact with someone who's kind. So be kind to your partner and inspire him or her.

Lane C., Eugene, Oregon

Warning: kindness is catching

Kindness is a huge issue for me. I love doing the little things to take care of my husband Bobby and in return he does the same for me.

For example, I'm a stay-at-home mom and I try to always make his lunch and serve him dinner when he's home. When he's off he always makes me breakfast. It's simple things like this but they make us feel cared for. It's a win-win situation.

An additional plus is that our small children are aware of it and are learning this behavior which will help them in their future relationships.

Marcia S., Bakersfield, California

After reading this chapter, test your relationship I.Q. with the **Improve Your Relationship QUIZ BOOK,** *then use the* **Improve Your Relationship WORK BOOK** *to work on the areas of your relationship that need a little help, using the simple action items checklist in the book. Both books are available only by visiting http://www.ImproveYourRelationship.com.*

#50: The Respect Rule

Unless you're like Rodney Dangerfield, and make your living from being disrespected, respect your partner's feelings, privacy, wishes and differences and you'll get the respect *you* deserve.

To take your relationship off the critical list, start by tossing your critical list

Respect is high on my list because it took a long time for me to get this concept. And, of course, I still struggle to remember to be respectful.

In the first years of our marriage I found myself constantly putting my husband Bobby down for all the things he wasn't doing right and really treating him worse than I would a dog, had I had one. It's sad that once you become familiar with someone it becomes so easy to take them for granted, and that's what I did. It really becomes a vicious cycle. I'd make him unhappy and then because he'd be unhappy, I'd be unhappy.

To turn it around I realized that if I showed more respect and appreciation he would too. For example, I now try to voice more often how much I appreciate all that he does, and he now does the same for me. Just being polite in life is a really big deal—it's nice to hear "thank you" often.

Marcia S., Bakersfield, California

Help your partner to respect him or herself and you'll both benefit

Growing up, I didn't think I was a very nice or good person. I'm not sure I even knew what love was when I met

Harry. I'm not even sure I was in love when I got married. But he was a wonderful human being who really loved me.

Because of him, I decided at this time to be the best me I could be. And that's what I did throughout our life together. Harry taught me about respect. He taught me never to criticize him in front of anyone. He also taught me to never let our sons work one of us against the other. If I told the boys they couldn't do something and Harry thought I was too stern he would call me in the other room and ask me to please change my mind and not be so hard on them.

Harry respected me and I learned to respect myself. I think I got the best part of the deal and I loved him dearly once I found out what love was all about.

Lillian S., San Jacinto, California

Give respect the respect it's due

In our society we no longer value respect. The church has become more scandalous than a daytime soap opera, cops are caught regularly beating motorists, corporate CEOs are led away in handcuffs on a regular basis, Presidents are impeached for infidelity, and it's all captured and played out on TV and in the tabloids, which are pretty much the same thing anymore.

If you let it, the world will gladly disrespect to. It's up to you to make sure you're treated with respect. Let your partner know that you will not tolerate being treated disrespectfully and he will respect you. You do this by being true to your word, by doing what you say you will do, and by holding fast to your convictions and following through.

My husband Glenn and I were brought up in a time, not too long ago, in which respect was valued. You didn't have to ask your partner for respect. Today you do. We respect our marriage vows and we respect each other's rights, feelings and decisions. We may not always agree with each other's choices but we respect them.

You can't have a happy relationship if you don't have respect for yourself and your partner. And contrary to popular opinion, you don't have to earn it—it's your right. But these days you do have to ask for it, and if necessary, demand it. Otherwise you may not get it.

Rebecca F., Washington, D.C.

If you want him to respect you in the morning

Respect seems to be one of the hardest things to get in a relationship. More than anything else, most of my friends complain that they don't feel respected by their partners.

I've found that the easiest way to get your partner to respect you is to start by respecting your partner—their opinions, their feelings, their decisions, and their wishes. It sounds simple but it isn't.

All of us want to be respected by our partners, but few of us want to give the same respect in return and that's where the problems start. It's not easy to respect someone who's not treating you with respect so you wind up in a stalemate.

You can turn around, but you have to make the first move. Only after you've made the first move and have shown that you respect your partner, can you request, and if you have to, demand that your wishes, desires and independence also be respected. It's not easy to stick to your guns, but if you do you'll be respected by any decent and respectable partner.

Lisa T., Atlanta, Georgia

After reading this chapter, test your relationship I.Q. with the **Improve Your Relationship QUIZ BOOK,** *then use the* **Improve Your Relationship WORK BOOK** *to work on the areas of your relationship that need a little help, using the simple action items checklist in the book. Both books are available only by visiting http://www.ImproveYourRelationship.com.*

#51: The Time / Priorities Rule

Make time for each other or you may be alone the next time you have time. Ask your partner out on a date at least once a week. A weekly date keeps a happy mate.

Pull the plug on your prime-time relationship melodrama

Is your relationship like a soap opera? If your mate prefers prime-time comedies or family fare, then it might be time to pull the plug on your melodrama or to sign up for a satellite dish so you can receive better channels.

For years I nagged and complained that my husband Colby was never around. Then one day a friend of mine told me that she couldn't be around me for an extended amount of time either. She said my life was too full of trauma and drama for her. Everything was a crisis or an issue with me.

At first I was insulted and rationalized and justified my behavior. I even blamed Colby. If he were only home more then there wouldn't be so much drama. But what she said struck a nerve with me and eventually I had to admit that she was right. I asked Colby if he agreed with my friend and, of course, he did.

He wasn't staying away from home because he really wanted to work all the time, it was just more pleasant than being at home in the middle of all the trauma. It was tough for me to accept that I was a major drama Queen. But I wanted my King around more and if that meant I had to lose the drama, then I was willing to abdicate.

Sometimes all it takes is for a trusted friend to knock you off your throne with the truth for you to see yourself the way others see you.

Debra R., Salem, Oregon

It's never to late to start dating your mate

Even after being married 39 years, we still plan dates like we did as a young, unmarried couple.

Our interests have changed over the years. Instead of a nightclub we go to a book store coffee shop where we have our night out. We might go to a lecture together. We also go to evening dances sponsored by our Community Center.

Our favorite date is to take a trip. My husband and I both drive, but we enjoy leaving the cars and taking the bus. We go on bus trips sponsored by local groups. The trips include lunch out. Sometimes they're day trips, other times they're overnight.

We try to have at least one date a week. That is, one day or night that we plan just for ourselves.

Bea S., Manchester, Connecticut

Make Monday through Sunday night special

Every Friday night my husband Josh and I have a standing date. We've been married 12 years and have only had to miss a date or two in all those years. Our very first date was a blind date.

We met at a Chinese restaurant and we've just continued the tradition ever since. Every Friday night we pick up Chinese take-out, rent a romantic movie—preferably a romantic comedy—light the candles and spend the evening cuddling on the couch. This is our time. And no matter what has occurred during the week we know we always have Friday to look forward to—and to spend the end of the week in each other's arms.

Stephanie S., Houston, Texas

Forget waiting for Valentine's Day—Celebrate *Your* Day

My secret for a happy relationship is to simply make time for your partner. Although it's not easy, set aside your cares and make your mate feel that he's worth it—because he is.

We pick one day out of the week called OUR DAY. We go to a favorite restaurant or cook a favorite meal. We relax afterwards together in a bubble bath and often follow that with a massage.

Nina C., Brooklyn, New York

Don't take a vacation from your relationship

One of our secrets to a happy relationship is that we take two vacations each year—one with the family (we have three children) and one just for us. We've been married for 24 happy years because we've always made time for each other.

Amy C., Prescott, Arizona

After reading this chapter, test your relationship I.Q. with the **Improve Your Relationship QUIZ BOOK,** *then use the* **Improve Your Relationship WORK BOOK** *to work on the areas of your relationship that need a little help, using the simple action items checklist in the book. Both books are available only by visiting http://www.ImproveYourRelationship.com.*

Section 9
The Last Rule

Follow this simple rule if you want to
achieve Relationship Excellence

#52: The Break the Rules Rule

*Some rules are meant to be broken.
And sometimes you have to break the rules
in order to play your own game. Just make
sure you both agree to the new rules.*

If the old rules aren't working for the two of you, agree on new rules

My grandparents lived in separate cities, 100 miles apart, but we're very happy together until the day they died. My grandfather was 15 years older than my grandmother and retired early from a military career.

My grandmother loved her job and was in no hurry to retire. So, he moved to their retirement home in the desert, and she stayed in their city home during the week and spent weekends with him at their desert retreat. They always seemed very much in love and this unconventional arrangement seemed normal to me as I grew up. It's also made it easier for me to have a non-traditional lifestyle with my partner, which has been a key to our happy twelve-year relationship.

Stuart J., Lexington, Kentucky

Like real estate, love is sometimes all about location, location, location

On paper, my husband David and I appear to be a perfect match. The reality is quite another matter. We love each other very much, but have never been able to live with one another for any length of time, under the same roof. He loves cats and

I'm allergic. When we're home, he likes to have the TV on in every room. I like a tranquil environment where I can meditate and do yoga. He's a slob and a pack rat. I'm a neat freak.

After a year living together it was obvious we couldn't live together, even though we were very much in love. Our solution was unconventional, to say the least. When the home next door went on the market, we purchased it. We stayed married but I moved to the new house. We've lived next door to one another for nine years now and have never been happier.

Who says you have to live in the same house just because you're married? Even stranger, is that we've met other couples over the years with similar arrangements. Sometimes you have to go against convention and tradition and do what works for you, and forget what the neighbors say.

Ivana M., Newark, New Jersey

Are you cheating yourself and your partner?

For most couples, infidelity is grounds for divorce. For us, it's grounds for a happy relationship. My wife Leah and I are very sexual people and believe that variety is the spice of life— and relationships. We're also very secure with ourselves and each other and believe jealousy is a result of being closed and fearful, not a result of openness.

We agreed before we were married that we would have an open marriage. Meaning we could have outside sexual encounters. The only stipulation is that we agreed we'd have to follow a few rules. We agreed to only have sex with other couples and to always do it together. That way there are no secrets and no chance it will turn into anything more. We also practice safe sex only. We know it's unconventional, but we believe for us, our open relationship has strengthened our love and our romantic life.

I guess most people would call us swingers, though we don't like to label ourselves that way. We just think of ourselves as being open to the entire sexual banquet of life, while at the same time having a loving, committed and very happy relationship. Why eat cranberry sauce exclusively for the rest of your life when the entire turkey dinner is available?

Society has separated marriage from sexual variety, but we don't see any reason to. For us, this has been one of the not-so-secret secrets to our long and happy relationship.

Lance L., Savannah, Georgia

How to avoid marriage-by-default

We've been very happy after cohabiting for eight years and I'd say the most important thing in our relationship is clear communication about the life we want to live together. We don't assume gender roles or take the default life plan (marriage, followed by children, followed by retirement, etc.); we talk about what we actually want from life together and make our own rules.

Sidelia R., Oxford, Ohio

After reading this chapter, test your relationship I.Q. with the **Improve Your Relationship QUIZ BOOK,** *then use the* **Improve Your Relationship WORK BOOK** *to work on the areas of your relationship that need a little help, using the simple action items checklist in the book. Both books are available only by visiting http://www.ImproveYourRelationship.com.*

Section 10
The Next Step

Have you ever read a self-improvement how-to book and felt you learned something but then forgot everything you learned a week or two later?

That's the problem with most self-help books; they're a lot like Chinese food, they're great, but they don't stay with you very long.

For those of you who found the tips, suggestions and advice on the previous pages helpful and now actually want to *do* something to improve *your* relationship, start by turning this page.

Where do I start?

If there were a Rule # 53 it would be
"The Action Rule." You start to improve *your*
relationship by *doing* something. If what you try
doesn't work, do something else until you
find something that does work.

Okay, so now what?

Now that you've read the 52 relationship rules and all of the advice and examples, you may be asking yourself, "So, how do I improve *my* relationship?" "What do I do now, where do I start?"

Start by by asking yourself these questions:

1. Which of the 52 relationship rules am I successfully playing by?
2. Which of the 52 relationship rules is my partner successfully playing by?
3. Which of the 52 relationship rules do I need to work on to be successful?
4. Which of the 52 relationship rules does my partner need to work on to be successful?

If you're not sure how to answer any or all of these questions, pick up my "52 Simple Rules to Improve Your Relationship QUIZ BOOK" and see how you score on each of the 52 relationship quizzes. Have your partner do the same and compare your scores.

The QUIZ BOOK is very simple to use. There are 52 rules and 52 quizzes. Each quiz is made up of 10 questions. After answering each question you total your score at the bottom of the page and discover if you are successfully playing by the rules or if you need some help.

After you've completed your quizzes, ask your partner to take the quizzes. Again, there are 52 rules and 52 quizzes for your partner. And again, each quiz is made up of 10 questions to help your partner discover if he or she is successfully playing by the rules or needs some help.

Next, take action using a simple, proven and easy-to-follow step-by-step guide

Once you both know which areas of your relationship you need to work on, you may then want to use my "52 Simple Rules to Improve Your Relationship WORKBOOK" to take the next, and most important step.

The WORKBOOK is also divided into 52 sections, one for each simple rule. Simply work on the rules you've identified as needing help and ignore the others.

Within each section there are four action items or exercises you need to take to improve your relationship. The WORK-BOOK walks you through each action item in an easy, step-by-step format.

You and your partner may want to work through the book daily, weekly, or monthly. You can work at your own pace, knowing that each action item will improve your relationship, each small but important step of the way.

Once you and your partner have completed each action item for the rules you've chosen to work on, you will have in writing a record of what you have done and the progress you've made.

The best thing about this WORKBOOK, besides the fact that it will improve your relationship, is that you and your partner will have the peace of mind that comes from knowing you've made every possible effort to create a win/win relationship for you and your partner.

If, after reading the RULE BOOK, the QUIZ BOOK and completing the WORKBOOK exercises you don't feel that your relationship has improved dramatically, please send all three books back to me for a complete refund at any time. That's how sure I am that these books will help you have a happier relationship.

These three books are based on the advice of thousands of happy couples. Their simple, fundamental and universal advice has been proven to work time and time again.

For those of you with bigger problems that aren't helped by the advice in these books, you may want to seek appropriate therapy or other professional assistance. But even then the books will be useful because you'll know you've done everything possible before taking that next important step. You may even want to share your WORKBOOK with your therapist so that he or she knows what you've already tried.

The advice offered in this book is shared in the spirit of hope, inspiration and entertainment and is not intended to take the place of a therapist, psychologist, psychiatrist, medical doctor, lawyer or other professional trained in these areas.

All of the advice, tips, hints, suggestions, solutions and opinions about sex, love, romance and relationship problems offered in this book is strictly the opinions of the individual contributors.

Contributors' advice is based on personal experience that worked for them but may not work for you. Again, please return this book for a full refund and/or consult a professional if you find any of the advice to be unhelpful or harmful in any way.

For those of you with normal, everyday relationship problems, you may want to begin the WORKBOOK with an easy rule, one in which you have only minor differences, and then work your way up to rules in which you have larger differences and obstacles to overcome. As you succeed in easier areas, your confidence will grow, allowing you to tackle more difficult obstacles.

Complete the WORKBOOK together and treat it like a game. This is a practical guide that's intended and designed to be a lot of fun, not a lot of work—in spite of the title.

If this series of practical books works for you I'd love to hear your success stories. If they don't work for you and you have suggestions for improvement, I'd love to hear from you, as well. Feel free to e-mail me at:

email@ImproveYourRelationship.com

Finally, to paraphrase 17th century scientist Isaac Newton's Third Law of Motion, "For every action, there's an equal and opposite reaction."

Newton probably wasn't referring to relationships, but his law still applies. If you want to improve your relationship—do something!

About the Author

Steve Stewart has been writing about sex, love and relationships for more than 20 years.

Stewart was born and raised not far from Hollywood, California, where he learned at an early age that to live happily ever after you need to do the opposite of what they do in the movies.

He began writing about movies and sexuality while in college and today his articles appear regularly in dozens of newspapers, magazines and web sites world wide.

A best-selling author, Stewart has written 17 books including *52 Simple Rules to Improve Your Relationship*, *The 52 Simple Rules Quiz Book*, *The 52 Simple Rules Workbook*, *From Hollywood With Love*, *The Full-Frontal Movie Guide*, *Out on the Screen*, *The Campy, Vampy, Trampy Movie Quote Book* and *Penis Puns*.

Stewart is still a movie buff and when he's not with his partner of 12 years, or with his grown daughter and his two grandchildren, you can find him at the movies.

To read an online interview with Stewart, please visit http://www.ImproveYourRelationship.com.

Free Relationship Tips Newsletter!

Visit our new web site today and sign-up to receive our FREE *Relationship Tips* e-newsletter. Share a sex, love, romance or relationship tip that we can use in our newsletter or books and you may even see yourself published. No purchase necessary. Visit http://www.ImproveYourRelationship.com for complete details. And while you're there, find out how you can receive FREE shipping and handling if you make a purchase.

http://www.ImproveYourRelationship.com

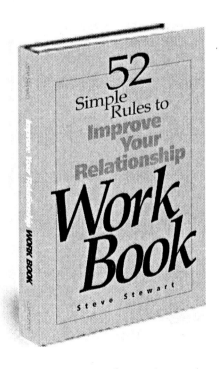

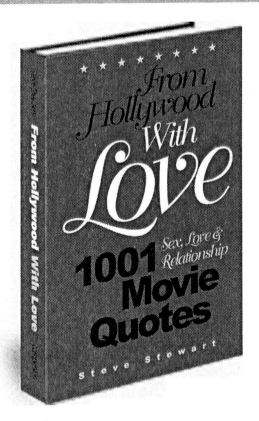

companion press sex, love & relationship books

52 Simple Rules to Improve
Your Relationship
Tips, Suggestions & Advice
From Couples Who Have
By Steve Stewart
224 pages, 5-1/2 x 8-1/8
ISBN: 1-889138-30-4
$15.95 Softcover

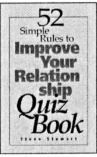

52 Simple Rules to Improve
Your Relationship
QUIZ BOOK
By Steve Stewart
224 pages, 5-1/2 x 8-1/8
ISBN: 1-889138-31-2
$15.95 Softcover

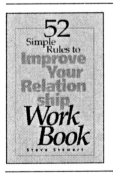

52 Simple Rules to Improve
Your Relationship
WORKBOOK
By Steve Stewart
224 pages, 5-1/2 x 8-1/8
ISBN: 1-889138-32-0
$15.95 Softcover

From Hollywood, With Love
1001 Sex, Romance &
Relationship Movie Quotes
By Steve Stewart
224 pages, 5-1/2 x 8-1/8
ISBN: 1-889138-24-X
$15.95 Softcover

You don't need
to be a movie
buff to enjoy
this book.
Also makes a
wonderful gift!

See Order Form on Next Page

companion press order form

PO Box 2575, Laguna Hills, CA 92654   USA

Phone: (949) 362-9726   Fax: (949) 362-4489

**Please include your phone number or <u>E-MAIL ADDRESS</u>
(for questions about your order):**

_____

PRINT Name _____

Address _____

City _____ State _____ Zip _____

PLEASE PRINT CLEARLY. USE EXTRA SHEET OF PAPER IF NECESSARY

Qty	Title	Price (each)	Price

SHIPPING & HANDLING CHARGES—BOOKS ONLY
U.S. <u>Shipping & Handling Charges</u> (U.S. ONLY)
First book $4.00. $1.00 for each additional book.
Canada <u>Shipping & Handling Charges</u> (Canada)
First book $5.00. $1.00 for each additional book.
Outside U.S. <u>Shipping & Handling Charges</u> (Outside U.S.)
First book $20.00. $1.00 for each additional book.
RUSH <u>FedEx Delivery Charges</u> (U.S. ONLY)
Check one and ADD to above charges ❏ Overnight, **Add** $35.00
❏ 2nd Day, **Add** $25.00 ❏ Saturday Delivery, **Add** $45.00.
CREDIT CARD or MONEY ORDERS ONLY for rush delivery.

Subtotal	$
Discount or Credit (if any)	-
California Residents add **7.75% Sales Tax**	$
Shipping & Handling **See left for rates**	$
ADD RUSH FedEx Delivery Charge	$
TOTAL	$

Check Payment Method
❏ Visa ❏ MasterCard ❏ American Express ❏ Money Order
❏ Check (U.S. only) **(Allow 6-8 weeks.)** Make check payable to COMPANION PRESS.

Credit card # _____ | Exp. date |_____

X Signature

_____

My signature here authorizes my credit card charge if I am paying for my order by Visa, MasterCard or American Express. We cannot ship your credit card order without your signature.

1/2003